With a style and historical perspective reminiscent of Belloc, Denis Meadows presents a sweeping view of the origin and growth of the Roman Catholic Church and its role in the world today.

This is the story of the Church resisting from ancient times the successive onslaughts of heresy, schism, internal corruption, barbarian invasion, Moslem expansion, communism, and domination by absolutists in the political world.

The great personalities of the Church are a living part of the story too: saints, reformers, pontiffs, founders of orders, scholars, and missionaries carrying the Gospel to all corners of the earth.

"I have had two objectives in mind," says the author, "in writing this book. The first was objectivity – adherence to the facts as I knew them. The second was frankness in dealing with shortcomings in the human beings who are members of the Church, whether lay or clerical."

The story of the Catholic Church has never before been told in such a short space by a writer of the eminence of Denis Meadows.

Jacket illustration: Christ, the Virgin, and saints, from Vatican manuscript of Christian Topography by Cosmas Indico-leustes, 6th-century Greek traveler and geographer.)

Born and educated in England, at Stonyhurst, Denis Meadows has lived for many years in the United States. He is the author of Tudor Underground (a Catholic Book Club and Catholic Family Book Club selection), Obedient Men (a Thomas More Book Club selection), A Popular History of the Jesuits, Elizabethan Quintet, and other books.

A Short History of the Catholic Church

A Short History
of the Catholic Church

DENIS MEADOWS

THE DEVIN-ADAIR COMPANY   NEW YORK   1959

Canadian agent: Thomas Nelson & Sons Ltd., Toronto
Library of Congress catalog card number: 59–13555
Designed by Walter Miles
Manufactured in the United States of America

Nihil obstat: Daniel F. Ryan, S.J., *Censor Deputatus*
                   June 20, 1959

Imprimatur: ✠Most Rev. Lawrence J. Shehan, D.D.
                   Bishop of Bridgeport
                   June 26, 1959

To My Wife

For Whom This Book Is Written

The phrase "church history," or the more forbidding term "ecclesiastical history," frightens many people away from books which ought to give them instruction and delight. They see in their mind's eye rows of volumes bound in shiny cloth or decaying leather, each containing hundreds of pages filled with the details of old heresies, half-forgotten quarrels between popes and emperors, and the complex discussions of church councils. The ordinary layman, the "general reader" for whom most authors and publishers work, cannot see the wood for the trees. He needs help to savor the true spirit of Catholic Church history.

The story of the Catholic Church, from the first Christian Pentecost in Jerusalem in 30 A.D. to our point of time in the twentieth century, is in fact a romance covering nearly two thousand years of mankind's history. Lord Macaulay, stout Whig and convinced Protestant, was aware of the fact. "There is not and there never was on this earth," he writes, "a work of human policy so well deserving of examination as the Roman Catholic Church." Then he adds, in words suggestive of the text about "the gates of hell," "When we reflect on the tremendous assaults which she has survived we find it difficult to conceive in what way she is to perish."

The story of the Catholic Church is then a romance, a true romance for Everyman, primarily for those whom it is generally agreed to call Roman Catholics, but not for them alone. The days are over, or nearly over, when, as Charles Williams puts it, "The normal calumnies of piety flew to and fro." The "other sheep, not of this fold," of whom Christ spoke, are, be it noted, *sheep,* not goats. The contemporary Roman Catholic, facing Marxist communism, thinks of his Protestant or Orthodox neighbor as a fellow Christian, not primarily as a "heretic" or "schismatic." For sixteen of its twenty centuries, anyhow, the story of the Church is simply that of the Judaeo-Christian heritage, with its Greek and Roman borrowings, on which our western way of life was built.

The Roman Catholic author, writing for his Protestant fellow Christians as well as for his brethren of the Roman obedience, has a special responsibility, that of sincerity, of candor in the face of scandals and abuses, at least equal to that of the skeptic or rationalist historian. Bad popes, worldly prelates, or venal churchmen merely confirm our belief in human free will; they do not disprove the claims of the Church. Even a deplorably high percentage of black sheep does not destroy the whiteness of the others in the flock, still less does it make us doubt the existence of the flock.

Contents

A Short History of the Catholic Church

1. Birth and Infancy of the Church

1. There is a foreshadowing of the establishment of the Church and its form of government in Christ's commission to Simon Peter as recorded in two of the four Gospels (Matt. 16:17-19 and John 21:15-17). "Feed my sheep" and "Feed my lambs," Christ commanded. St. Matthew records that He used the Aramaic form of the Apostle's name to assert that *Peter* was the *rock* whereon would be founded a Church against which "the gates of hell" should not prevail. Attempts have been made in controversy to prove this text an interpolation. The details are out of place in a book that aims neither at controversy nor apologetics and that seeks only to tell a story straightforwardly and as sincerely as possible.

We may pass on, then, to the year which is generally accepted—30 A.D. In the first chapter of the Acts of the Apostles we read an account of what we may call the birthday of the Church. It was a momentous event; next to the crucifixion and the resurrection of Christ it is, to the Catholic believer, the most momentous thing in man's history. All who call themselves Christians take account of that first Christian Pentecost. The churches which have developed a fixed liturgy and a ritual celebrate the event with impressive services, the Eastern Orthodox Church even more elaborately than Rome herself.

Let us, however, see that gathering in Jerusalem on the day of Pentecost in the perspective of history. Those followers of Christ, who had been dismayed by the Master's death on the cross and then made exultant by His resurrection, were Jews, orthodox, observant of the Mosaic law; they were not even called Christians as yet. Most of them had at first looked on their Master as the King of the Jews, king in a mundane sense, who would liberate them from the Romans and set up a flourishing Hebrew nationalism. By now their minds had moved beyond that naïve dream and they looked to an early second coming such as, in the Middle Ages, Thomas of Celano described in the hymn *Dies Irae* of requiem Masses—Christ a king in more than earthly glory, judging all men, allotting eternal reward or punishment and closing the final chapter of man's history on the earth.

To those first Christian believers their Lord had indeed spoken of His universal mission, commanding His disciples to evangelize all nations, but as yet the concept expressed by the word *Catholic,* borrowed later from Greek, was at best latent in their minds.

In Jerusalem was assembled the Christian Church—Christ's Virgin Mother, the headstrong, passionate Simon Peter to whom had been committed the keys of the new Kingdom, ten others of the original twelve, and one Matthias, recently elected by ballot to replace the apostate Judas. In addition to these—the Church's mother and patroness and its first hierarchy—were other faithful disciples, making up a total of about a hundred and twenty people, says the author of the Acts of the Apostles. Then came the outpouring of what theologians call divine grace. The descent of the Holy Spirit on the twelve Apostles was symbolized by the parted tongues, as it were of

4

fire. The bystanders, of various languages, Jews from many regions of the Near East, heard the new Faith proclaimed, seemingly in all their different languages, by a group of Galilean provincials. And the effect on these bystanders? Amazement and a wondering awe in some cases, but others mocked, saying the men were drunk with the product of the new vintage. Then Peter, his primacy clearly recognized by his brethren, stood with the other eleven Apostles around him and addressed the crowd. He denied the charge of drunkenness and preached the infant Church's first sermon of Christian propaganda. Many consciences were touched, some, it may be, of those that had at first mocked and jeered. When the day of Pentecost came to an end, three thousand converts had been baptized, the first fruits of a missionary effort which still continues.

With fervor and an eloquence that owed nothing to the Greek and Latin teachers of rhetoric the Galilean fisherman preached in his rustic accent Christ crucified and risen. The apostle spoke as a Jew to Jews, the "men of Israel," whose racial stock and whose ancestral religion were his own. It was to them and their offspring that he offered the "gospel" or good news of a spiritual order that made the old dispensation obsolete by completing it and fulfilling its prophecies. Peter did indeed speak of those that are afar off, and of as many as God shall call unto Himself, but his words did not as yet point unmistakably to a world-wide Christian mission, addressing itself equally to Jews and Gentiles, freemen and slaves, intellectual Hellenists, practical, empire-governing Romans, and the obscure, anonymous millions who are the Common Men of all ages.

Only gradually and not without argument and even friction among brethren did the idea of Catholicity, that is universality, come to dominate the minds of the early Jewish Christians and set the pattern for their future work. From the second century onward the word *Catholic* was in general use by Christian writers.

Peter saw undeniable evidence that in non-Jewish souls the Holy Spirit was at work, and he fraternized and ate with men who had not submitted to the rite of circumcision or embraced the form of worship enjoined by Judaism. Even Peter, however, needed a dream or vision of the essential goodness of all God's creatures to show him that the Old Law, with its exclusiveness, its dietary laws, and its burden of ritual observance, was indeed replaced by a new mode of life and thought. Of this the keynote was simply charity or love, the twofold love of God and His creature man which Christ preached, as forming the two great commandments.

Already, in the first century of the infant Church, we can pick out three strands or threads which are going to run through the whole skein of Catholic history. There will, of course, from time to time be worldly and self-seeking prelates, lazy and sensual priests, unworthy popes —worst scandal of all, two and at times three claimants to the supreme authority of Peter's Chair—but always, under varying circumstances and in varying degrees, three aspects of the life of the Church can be traced in her long history.

There is, first of all, her consciousness of a missionary vocation, the task allotted her by her Founder to spread the Faith, to teach it to all mankind, not merely to preserve it.

Secondly, we observe the thing we call martyrdom. The word *martyr,* of Greek origin, means simply a witness, but we have come to limit the term to the supreme and ultimate witness any human being can give, namely, testimony sealed with his lifeblood. For our present purpose, however, we may widen the use of the word to embrace the higher kinds of holy living, and dying, even when they do not comprise physical torture and a violent death. A very little reading of the lives of holy men and women will show us that suffering in some form or other has been always a part of the witness which sanctity bears to the Faith.

In the third place we shall view the achievements through the early period of the Church's life of those whom historians call the Christian apologists. Here, again, we need to be clear about the meaning of the word we use. Apology, as a shamefaced acknowledgment of error or wrongdoing, is a comparatively modern meaning of the term. *Apologia,* from the Greek through Latin, was a defense and explanation of truth as the writer saw it, his use of his distinctively human faculty, reasoning power, to make clear and acceptable to his fellowmen something he held to be of profound importance. A good example in modern times would be Cardinal Newman's *Apology for His Life* (if we translate the Latin literally). That classic of religious autobiography is no confession of wrongdoing. It is a defense and justification of all that led up to an act of right doing, the sacrifice of a career and of cherished affections when the writer made his submission to Rome. The book was by implication, we may note, a crushing answer to the attacks of the Reverend Charles Kingsley.

Such documents, apologias that are both defense and attack, will come to our notice with increasing frequency as we see the Church growing in membership and influence and as she is able to broaden her attack on what we call heresy. The rise of heresies and the unceasing fight of the Church against them form another part of her two-thousand-year story. *Heresy* is another of the words Christian theology has taken from the Greek, from a verb meaning "to choose." A heretic is one who picks and chooses among the articles of faith, accepting those he likes and rejecting others or substituting for them his own opinions or explanations.

2. We may now consider in more detail these three aspects of the life and work of the early Church. As we do so we should note that they formed a pattern which has lasted for twenty centuries and which, so far as we can see, will continue so long as mankind dwells on this planet. We start, then, with the missionary vocation of the Church which began on that day of Pentecost recorded in the Acts of the Apostles. To the embryo Church of one hundred and twenty persons were added, we are told, about three thousand converts as the result of two things, the visible signs of the descent of the Holy Spirit and the preaching of St. Peter.

About seven years later, that is, in 36 or 37 A.D., came the event which was to sweep away any lingering belief that the preaching of the new Faith was to be restricted to the Jewish people. Connected with this event, the conversion of Saul of Tarsus to the St. Paul of Christian history, is the first witness to the Christian Faith by martyrdom, the deacon Stephen. Saul, who had Roman citizenship in virtue of his birth in a colony affiliated to the Roman Empire, was an orthodox Jew. Indeed, he was a Jew of the Jews, a zealot engaged in the inquisitorial task of hunting down and persecuting as subversives the followers of the Revolutionary whom a Roman proconsul, under pressure from the Jewish hierarchy, had sentenced to a criminal's death by crucifixion. Stephen, a deacon or assistant in the administrative and philanthropic work of the Christian community, was stoned to death by a fanatical mob. "Saul," the book of Acts tells us briefly, "was consenting unto his death." The story of the persecutor Saul's journey to Damascus, of his temporary blindness and of the voice from heaven rebuking him for his ruthless and misguided zeal is told vividly in the same earliest volume of church history. After three days of blindness and of abstention from food and drink, Saul received his sight again through the agency of a Christian in Damascus. From now on he becomes Paul, the Apostle of the Gentiles, founder of churches, theologian, mystic, and finally, after a quarter of a century of missionary travel, preaching, writing, controversy, and vicissitudes of all kinds, a martyr for the Christian faith in Rome itself.

The intense zeal of the recent persecutor for making converts among non-Jews—insisting only on faith in the Christian teaching and acceptance of the sacrament of baptism—was looked at askance by some of the more conservative of his co-religionists. They could not at first accept the idea that circumcision and all the other obligations of Judaism were now obsolete. About the year 50 A.D., however, the whole matter was threshed out in a Council or meeting of church rulers in Jerusalem. Whatever he had been before his conversion, St. Paul showed himself wise and generous in controversy. With the principle admitted that Gentile converts were admissible to the Church without going through a probationary stage of Judaic practice, including circumcision, Paul willingly made concessions which would please traditional Jewish sentiment; we might almost say traditional prejudice. The converts should observe certain dietary laws—against "things strangled and blood," laws clearly obsolete when St. Peter had been shown in a vision that God's creation had nothing "common or unclean" in it.

From that time onwards the story of the Catholic Church is to be largely a record of missionary activity. There are, to start with, the missionary journeys of St. Paul himself and it is no exaggeration to say that the record of them in the Acts of the Apostles forms a Christian adventure story of enthralling interest. Much of the work of Christian propaganda in the earliest period was carried on by traveling missionaries whose very names are unknown to us. That this work did go on and that it met with much success we know from the steady growth of the body of believers and the early rise of "churches"—assemblies of the faithful—in all parts of the known world. That world was approximately the region over which the Roman Empire exercised control, an area originally limited to the lands bordering the Mediterranean and then extending gradually to the north, south, and east. Before long the pioneers of Christian missionary work outstripped the Roman empire builders. A persistent tradition, for example, places the founding of a Christian church in India in apostolic times. Of details of the life and religious practice of these early Christians, whether in Europe or beyond it, we know only too little. The book of the Acts of the Apostles tells us of a voluntary community of goods in the Church in Jerusalem. The more fervent converts, it may be, pooled their money and their labors for the general welfare, much as monks and nuns were to do somewhat later. That there was a high level of altruism and what we now call charitable work, we know from the constant references to almsgiving and from the fact that deacons had to be appointed just for this work, so that the fully ordained priesthood might be left free for directly religious duties. We know, too, that a commonplace of pagan observers, looking on with bewilderment or even hostility at the new religion, was "See how these Christians love one another!"

Theologians, who have orderly minds, like to consider the Church in three phases or stages of her life as she advances towards the consummation willed by her Founder. There is, first, the Church Militant, fighting against sin, error, and scandal on this earth. Then we have the Church Suffering, a sequel to the first phase and also contemporary with it. It is the life beyond the grave known as Purgatory, the life of souls redeemed and assured of ultimate happiness but still with a debt of temporal punishment to be paid. Lastly, there is the Church Triumphant, consisting of the faithful enjoying the Beatific Vision: in everyday language, heaven. We are concerned only with the Church Militant now, but it is necessary to keep in mind that the Church on this earth is a suffering as well as a fighting church, for persecution has never wholly ceased. Indeed, as we look around today we have no reason to foresee a future of halcyon calm, with persecution only a thing in the history books.

Following the practice of both Catholic and Protestant scholars, we consider the first three centuries of our era as covering the infancy of the Church, known variously as "primitive Catholicism" and "the early Church." It starts logically with what we have called the Church's birthday, Pentecost, 30 A.D., and it is closed by Constantine's victory at the Milvian Bridge in 312, followed the next year by the Edict of Milan, which ended the persecutions.

The first persecution of Christians may be said to start with the martyrdom of St. Stephen. The Jews, except for the small number who had accepted Christ's Messiahship, would have been glad to exterminate His followers. The Jews, however, were a subject race, governed by a centralized empire wherein the officials and the intellectuals tended to regard all religions with a tolerant skepticism. The Romans' real god was the omnicompetent state—a point of view only too familiar to us nowadays. Moreover, the Jews' fierce nationalism soon brought about the end even of colonial nationhood. After years of turbulence and restlessness, marked by atrocities on both sides, they were utterly crushed in 70 A.D. Jerusalem was occupied and sacked and the Temple was burned.

After the fall of Jerusalem the Romans treated Jews, in matters of religion as distinct from nationality, with tolerant contempt. They were required to make the approved gestures of worship and sacrifice to the deified emperor or else be treated as subversives. The Christian refused to render to Caesar the things that are God's. This led to the series of persecutions which, with intervals of mildness and even of toleration, took place in the period of nearly two and a half centuries between the reign of Domitian and Constantine's military victory.

The state of mind of pagan Rome in the early age of the Church must be taken into account if we are to explain the continuance and severity of persecution. The Romans regarded the Christian community as an obscure offshoot of Judaism, and the Empire normally was tolerant of all manner of cults brought into the capital from the Near East. The educated Roman, as we know from passages in Latin literature, did not accept the proletariat's anti-Christian stories of cannibal rites, child murder, and so forth, nor was he necessarily repelled by Christian teaching if he knew anything about it. He thought it foolish rather than evil. His complaint against these people was not that they worshiped false gods or indulged in abominable rites but that they were atheists. He meant that they rejected the polytheism of the state religion and that they opposed recognition of the *numen* or divine character of the Head of the State. In a phrase, he thought them bad citizens.

Unless we are clear about this, we shall not understand the paradox that the best emperors were, with several striking exceptions, the worst persecutors. The otherwise admirable record of Marcus Aurelius, who died in 180 A.D., is stained by a bitter persecution of the Christians. This virtuous pagan, surnamed the Philosopher, seems to have been an *anima naturaliter Christiana* (a spirit close to Christianity by natural goodness), and it is sad to see him enforcing the torture and execution of Christians. To a good Roman, polytheism was the established Church and he saw hostility to it as a form of treason.

Of the many thousands of Christians, men, women, and sometimes children just old enough to understand the

Faith, we know only a minority by name and little about most of those. There were at intervals the unhappy apostates, who were broken by terror or physical agony and made the required token sacrifice. The conformist thus brought to heel received his *libellus* or government paper to prove his loyal citizenship. Such *libellatici*, even when they had done no more than bribe an official to issue the document, were looked on with aversion by their fellow believers, and only by long and rigorous penance could they hope to regain the trust of the other Christians. There were, indeed, some clerics so severe that they regarded the rehabilitation of a *libellaticus* as impossible.

With intervals of relative peace, then, the infant Church was for over two and a half centuries a proscribed body, whose members met in secret for worship, instruction, and the sacraments in the mazelike underground cemeteries we call the Catacombs. Christians revealing their religion by word or action were in danger of betrayal to the authorities, followed by arrest. Then would come the choice between apostasy and death, often a lingering one. Like all outlawed minorities, they evolved a technique for secrecy, including the sign of the fish, casually doodled with forefinger or sandaled toe, which served to identify a fellow believer.* When the Church came out of the Catacombs, she was free to worship and to evangelize the pagans who, like the restless spirits in Virgil's underworld, were stretching out their hands in unconscious love of the further shore. The martyrs had borne their witness; the story of their heroism aided the work of proselytism. In that sense Tertullian spoke when he said the blood of martyrs was the seed of the Church.

---

* The Greek word for a fish ('ιχθύς) had been adopted because it was made up of the initial letters of the phrase, in Greek, *Jesus Christ, Son of God, Savior.*

3. As the Church grew in size and influence, it was not enough that Christians should have borne witness with their lifeblood. Christian intellectuals had an obligation to see if they could by persuasion and teaching move their pagan fellowmen towards the study of the new religion. The written word was the instrument to be used. In the phase of Catholic life that followed the age of the apostles and martyrs, we shall see this movement reaching its fruition in the works of the Greek and Latin Fathers of the Church. During the early Christian centuries a number of the "apologists" were martyrs as well as writers, thus leaving for posterity a twofold witness to the Faith.

The chief value of these early Christian writers to us moderns is their testimony to the beliefs of the early Church. To read them with an open mind is to pierce through the fog of controversy and discern a primitive Church recognizably the same as that of the Middle Ages, of the reforms of Trent, and of Pope John XXIII.

The earliest apologists were mostly converts from paganism, educated in the philosophy of their time, that of the Greeks. They were able as well as anxious to show that much of what was best in pre-Christian thought was in line with the new gospel. This work of Christian apologetics, presenting the unchangeable doctrines of the Church in the idiom of successive ages in a tradition, we can trace from the earliest times through the Church Fathers of the fourth and fifth centuries, the scholastics of the Middle Ages (especially St. Thomas Aquinas), and, reinvigorated, in our own time by such writers as Gilson and Maritain.

Of these early apologists we may take two as appealing to us by a certain modernity in their attitude. Both of them, too, are of those who were faithful unto death. The first of these, St. Justin, or Justin Martyr, was born about 100 A.D., within a lifetime, that is, of the birth of the Church at Pentecost. His parents were pagans, citizens of the Empire, but Greek-speaking provincials whose home was in Syria. After his conversion, probably when he was about thirty years old, he wandered about the Near East, earning his living by his lectures. Intellectual alertness had been stimulated, not stifled, by his conversion and he was eager to reconcile all that was best in the thought of his day with the Christian teaching. His confidence that this could be done led him to dedicate his *Apology* to the persecuting philosopher-emperor Marcus Aurelius. Another of his known books is a *Dialogue* with a Jewish friend, Trypho. Justin knew the Old Testament prophets as well as the Greek philosophers, and he uses his knowledge to reconcile the Old Testament with the new gospel. At some time in his adult life Justin made his way to Rome and settled there. We hear of him as an elderly philosopher, with a lecture room in which he taught and wrote. He was probably in his sixties when he was betrayed to the state officials, by a jealous rival according to one report, and was executed because he would not renounce Christianity.

Let us take St. Irenaeus as the second of our early apologists. He was bishop and martyr and, like St. Justin, his older contemporary, a provincial citizen of the Roman Empire. His home was in Asia Minor; he tells us of his listening in childhood to the sermons of St. Polycarp, bishop of Smyrna, which is the Izmir of the modern Turkish Republic. This bishop and certain elderly priests* in the neighborhood had known St. John, the

* From the earliest times the Christian Church recognized the distinction between *bishops,* exercising all the sacramental powers and the authority of the Twelve Apostles and conferring the powers and the authority on those whom they in turn consecrated, and the *priests* or presbyters. The priests had not the power to ordain other priests or to consecrate bishops, and their authority was, normally, limited to a smaller group, the origin of the later "parish." St. Peter (Acts 20:28) reminds the "elders" of the Church in Ephesus of their obligation to the flock wherein "the Holy Ghost hath made you bishops." The Greek word for *bishop* is ἐπίσκοπος ("overseer"), clearly implying administrative authority.

Beloved Disciple, so we have in Irenaeus a link with the very earliest days of the Christian religion. He was at work as a priest in the old French city of Lugdunum (Lyons) during the persecution under Marcus Aurelius. We hear of him at this time as a delegate to Rome, seeking from Pope Eleutherius support in a policy leading to the reconciliation of the Montanists and their return to orthodoxy. They formed a schism of puritans or rigorists in North Africa. When Irenaeus returned to Lyons he was elected by the Christians of the city to rule the diocese in place of the previous bishop, Pothinus, a victim of the persecution. He made many converts among the pagans and lived up to his name, Greek for "peacemaker," by smoothing the way for sectaries and schismatics to return to the Church. His fame as one of the earliest of the Catholic theologians rests on his book against the Gnostics, generally known by a Latin title, *Adversus Haereses* ("Against the Heresies"). In his attack on Gnosticism the bishop was dealing with a type of religious thought somewhat akin to the Modernism condemned fifty years ago by Pope St. Pius X, an emphasis on "intuition" as opposed to the literal acceptance of what the Church teaches. This spirit, in our time as in that of St. Irenaeus, tended towards the acceptance of all Christian dogma as symbolism only. What brings St. Irenaeus close to modern Catholic thinking is his insistence on the apostolic Roman See as the source and judge of what the Church teaches. Of the death of St. Irenaeus we have no further record than the statement of St. Gregory of Tours in the sixth century that he died as a martyr in the time of the Emperor Septimius Severus, at the end of the second century.

St. Justin, St. Irenaeus, and a number of other apologists and theologians who lived and, in many cases, died as martyrs in the first three centuries of the Church were often called upon for a twofold task. They sought to win converts by offering the sweet reasonableness of Christianity in contrast to the harshness of pagan belief and the bleak skepticism of the educated classes. Their second task was to combat the heresies or arbitrary doctrines of men who arose within the Church and threatened its apostolic teaching or its code of life. With the coming of Christian emperors, bodily persecution would cease, but the more subtle danger from false prophets would grow greater through the ages.

2. The Church and the Emperors

1. In the early part of the fourth century the Church came out of the Catacombs. She enjoyed freedom of worship and basked in the favor of the Empire's powerful ruler, the first Constantine. Were there, perhaps, optimists among the clergy and the faithful who thought that a Christian Golden Age, more glorious than that of Virgil, was about to open? If so, they had forgotten their Lord's promise of crosses and adversity. Temporarily, however, the new freedom was a blessing, for it enabled the Church to develop and perfect her government, to educate her children and, above all, to carry on her mission of spreading Christ's gospel. We must see how this sudden liberation came about and how it was destined to bring troubles as well as blessings upon the Church.

Christianity was growing steadily, in spite of the persecutions, all through the time when the Roman Empire, which had given peace and security under law to its world, was decaying. Edward Gibbon, the eighteenth-century British historian of the Roman Empire, would have us believe that the growth of the Christian Church was itself a factor in that decay. Some later historians have tried to revive Gibbon's judgment, but most have revised it. The decay had already started within a century and a half of the Crucifixion. Gibbon himself gives the year 180 A.D., that of the death of Marcus Aurelius, as the beginning of *The Decline and Fall* which is the subject of his masterpiece.

The early and middle years of the third century saw a rapid succession of emperors, a few of them good men by pagan standards, one admittedly a Christian, and one, Elagabolus (erroneously Latinized as Heliogabolus), a moral monster such as we seldom meet in real life. A period of violence and governmental anarchy, with military cliques putting their favorites on the throne and other cliques murdering them, was ended temporarily when Diocletian became emperor in 284. He was a clear-sighted administrator and saw that the Empire had become too big a thing for one man to rule efficiently. He appointed a co-ruler, Maximian, to share the burden. To each emperor was given an assistant; the senior was an *Augustus,* the assistant a *Caesar.* Diocletian, one of the "good" emperors, was responsible for the last systematic persecution of the Christians. It was also the bitterest and most ruthless, for its aim was the destruction of the new Faith. Diocletian is something of an enigma to the historian. His own wife and his daughter were Christians; left to himself he might have been tolerant enough in matters of religion, but he probably saw in the Church the one formidable rival which the Roman State, of which the Roman religion was a department, could never assimilate. Moreover, he was worked on by the pagan priesthood and by the conservative paganism of his soldiers. If the chronicles of the historian-bishop Eusebius, who died about 340 A.D., are reliable, the sufferings inflicted on the Christians under Diocletian rival all such things in the history of our world until we come to Hitler and Stalin.

Worn out by his labors, disillusioned by his failure with

economic problems and, perhaps, sickened by the horrors his religious policy had unleashed, he stepped down from his throne in 305 A.D., as did his co-ruler Maximian. He spent the eight years left to him in a palace on the coast of Illyria (Jugoslavia), growing vegetables as a hobby.

Anarchy again threatened the empire. The Caesars, the assistant emperors, had now become Augusti and fought among themselves for supremacy. The details of the struggle scarcely concerned the cruelly persecuted Church of Diocletian's last few years of rule. The momentous event was the final and complete victory of Constantine, one of the Caesars, over his last surviving rival in 312. On the eve of the battle, according to tradition, the still-pagan Constantine had a dream or vision of the Cross and with it the Greek words Ἐν τούτῳ νίκα—"In this conquer," or, according to some, the Latin words, *In hoc signo vinces*—"In this sign thou shalt conquer."

Two Augusti, Constantine in the east and Licinius in the west, now ruled the empire together. The year after the battle by the Tiber they met at Milan and passed the edict which established religious toleration throughout their territories. The Christian Church was now on the same footing as polytheism, Judaism, Mithraism (then very popular), and various oriental sects which had found their way to Rome. Nine years later the two emperors quarreled and in a battle Licinius was defeated. His life was spared at first, for his wife was Constantine's half-sister, but he was put to death later, on a charge of conspiring with the barbarians.

The Greek Orthodox Church reveres Constantine as a saint, but whatever his faith at the time of his great victory he postponed baptism until he was dying and then it was given him by a priest who was a heretic and a sectary. His first granting of toleration may have been chiefly a matter of policy, but he soon went beyond mere toleration. He rebuilt ruined Christian churches, restored property of the Church that had been sequestrated, and tacitly recognized the Catholic counsels of perfection by abolishing the civic penalty for celibacy. Also, as a mark of respect and perhaps a tribute to the humanity of the Christians, he did away with crucifixion as a statutory punishment.

One feature of his policy may have caused uneasiness in the minds of the clergy. His concessions to the believers, whose head was the Bishop of Rome, successor to St. Peter, were not extended to the various bodies of schismatic Christians already in existence. This was gratifying in one way, but disturbing in another. Here was a still-unbaptized ruler, with absolute power and, in the popular mind, connected with the old idea of the imperial *genius* or quasi-divine spirit, deciding what form of belief was acceptable to the head of the state and acting accordingly. This might some time prove to be a two-edged sword, for here was Caesar settling what belonged to God.

2. Within a decade of the Edict of Milan a new kind of trouble was brewing, more difficult to deal with than persecution because more subtle. This was the rise of new heresies, insidious because the outcome of apparent zeal or because of their appeal to the more educated Christians.

From New Testament times, when followers of Christ had left Him because of "hard sayings," heresies had arisen and led to the establishing of nonconforming bodies of Christians, rival churches in whose eyes the others were unenlightened. Especially in Romanized North Africa this thing repeatedly happened. Perhaps it can be explained as the effect of grafting the ardent, indigenous temperament on the Latin stock of the colonists. In Roman Africa, for example, arose Montanism, less a heresy than a schism of extremists, puritanical Christians whose leader, Montanus, based his whole teaching on a belief in the imminent second coming of Christ. The movement robbed the third-century Church of one of its ablest defenders, Tertullian. He is the founder of western theology, who had given the Church he abandoned her Latin tongue. It is not unreasonable to see him as the greatest of the Latin Fathers before St. Augustine, who appeared nearly two centuries later. The record of Tertullian's long life, his many controversies with pagans, and finally his break with the Church in which he had been an adult convert shows something we can find in so many of the great spiritual rebels—a haunting nostalgia for the spiritual home they had wandered from.

More formidable than any heresy or schism which came before it was the rise of Arianism in the fourth century. This heresy was an attack on the central point in Catholic belief, the two natures of Jesus Christ. Moreover, it is entangled with the question of the Roman emperor's authority in religious matters, a problem that was to harass churchmen for many centuries. Briefly, it may be said that Arianism denied the fullness of the Godhead in the person of Jesus Christ. The controvery bristled with subtleties, but the main issue was the Arian claim that Jesus Christ, as the second Person of the Trinity, was not "of the same substance" as the Father. He was "similar to, but not consubstantial with" the Father. Logically this undermines two basic Catholic doctrines—the Incarnation and the Redemption—and led to a kind of unitarianism. Perhaps the early followers of Arius, a popular and eloquent priest in Egypt, did not see the full implications of the master's teaching. Arius' bishop, however, did see the error in the new doctrine and denounced it, but Arius was backed by another bishop, Eusebius, a former fellow student, who held the important see of Nicomedia. Then began the great controversy waged by writings and sermons, episcopal condemnations and countercondemnations, the depositions of Catholic bishops and the thrusting of Arians into their sees and, at times, riots and tumults on the part of the laity. Constantine was alarmed by the threat to order and political stability. On his own authority he summoned the bishops of the Church to assemble in council and work out a formula to express the true teaching of the Church on the question in dispute.

The place chosen for the council was the town of Nicaea, in the northern part of Asia Minor, easily accessible from the Bosphorus, the Black Sea, and the Mediterranean. There, in 325 A.D., gathered some three hundred bishops. Those from eastern sees were in the majority, but—an important point for the Catholic historian— one of the presiding officials, along with the emperor himself, was a western bishop, Hosius, from distant Cordova. There were delegates, moreover, from the Roman pontiff, St. Sylvester I, and they were accorded precedence when it came to signing the final decrees.

This Council, whose name is enshrined in the *Nicene* Creed recited in the Mass of the Roman rite, is one of the landmarks in a long journey. That journey is the process by which the Church has worked out through the centuries an ever clearer and more detailed expression of the contents of the "deposit of faith" or body of truths left by Christ in the keeping of the Church founded on a Rock, St. Peter. To this process Cardinal Newman gave the name which served as the title of his book, *The Development of Doctrine.*

The outcome of the discussions of the Council of Nicaea can be stated briefly. The assembled fathers proclaimed the "consubstantiality" of the second Person of the Trinity with the first, in other words, God the Father and God the Son were of the same nature or "essence." The Arians were declared to be in error and were banished *by order of the emperor.* The italicized words foreshadow trouble to come, the struggle of the State to usurp the functions of the Church.

Probably Constantine, always busy with warfare, administration, and the exercise of far-reaching power, and still an unbaptized pagan, had little to do with the theology of the Council. He was concerned for order and unity in his empire. Unfortunately the leadership of Arius was followed after his death by that of an able bishop, his friend Eusebius of Nicomedia. This prelate was what in eighteenth-century England was called a trimmer, a politician skilled in compromise and the invention of noncommittal formulas. He dominated the mind of Constantine and persuaded him to support vague statements of Christian doctrine which betrayed the declaration of Nicaea. Thus it came about that the emperor's deathbed baptism, although valid, was performed by an Arian priest (337 A.D.).

Constantius, who succeeded his father, kept up the compromising "political" stand on religious matters. The eastern empire, so far as the higher clergy were concerned, had pretty well become an Arian state after ten years of Constantius' rule. The western emperor, Constans, was orthodox in doctrine, but his death by murder in 350 meant a temporary victory for Arianism. For a time the outlook was grim, and by 359 the Arians might well have hoped for a final conquest of men's minds in both east and west. A group of bishops of both empires was convened, meeting once in Italy and once in Asia Minor. The majority signed one of those ambiguous formulas which could be so interpreted as to undermine belief in the unity of God in a Trinity of Persons or which, on the other hand, might seem to accept the Incarnation in the Catholic sense.

Three years later, that is in 371, the Christian outlook became even grimmer. A nephew of Constantine, Flavius Claudius Julianus, whom we know as Julian the Apostate, became the western emperor. He was a tragic young ruler rather than the sinister Judas figure of popular legend. He had been baptized and, in early life, educated as a Christian of sorts, that is to say, by Arian palace eunuchs and under the influence of the Arian Bishop Eusebius of Nicomedia. Julian was a studious young man who, like many such, lived mentally in a romantic past that had never truly existed. His imaginative paradise was a high-minded, virtuous paganism, flourishing in a Golden Age that, as he saw it, had been succeeded by an age of Christian superstition having its source in a backward province on the eastern frontier of the empire. He was an earnest student of the ancient philosophers and dreamed of an ideal empire based on their teachings. He was probably the only person who truly believed in the kind of paganism he hoped to restore. He did not resort directly to the brutalities of earlier emperors, although he often allowed mob rule to have its way against the Christians. His method was more subtle. He sought to starve the Faith out of existence by depriving the Christians of churches and schools, stripping them of civic rights and economic freedom, and reopening the old pagan temples. The whole thing was short-lived, for after a reign of less than two years Julian was mortally wounded in battle and died in his tent. The story of his last words, *Vicisti, Galilæe!* ("Thou hast conquered, Galilean!") is of doubtful authenticity, but the words were a true forecast of the future.

Julian was succeeded by Catholic emperors who fought the advance of Arian teaching in the west. There was a brief revival of it in the east under Valens (364-378), but he was followed by Theodosius, a powerful ruler whose policy in church affairs was based on the teaching of the Roman pontiff. Meanwhile, however, we may ask ourselves, who raised his voice in behalf of the genuine apostolic belief in Christ's divinity during all those years of

Arian triumph? The answer is Athanasius, bishop of Alexandria. We come across many so-called great men in history, most of them evil, as Lord Acton remarked, but from time to time a nation or a church is blessed with a man who joins sanctity to the qualities of intellect and will that make for greatness as the world reckons it. Such as this was Athanasius. He was born about the end of the third century, almost certainly in Alexandria. We know little of his ancestry, but his education was in the best tradition of Christian Hellenism. Very early in his career he took part in the fight for orthodoxy against Arianism. As a young deacon he went with his bishop to the Council of Nicaea. The bishop nominated him as successor, according to the custom of the time. In 328 he was canonically appointed to the see despite Arian opposition. There is a story that crowds of the common people thronged the streets, crying out, "Give us Athanasius, the good, one of the ascetics." This is a reference to the future bishop's friendship with the Egyptian desert fathers and his enthusiasm for their ascetic spirituality. He is one of our sources of knowledge about the whole movement, and his life of St. Anthony is one of the early classics of religious biography.

The phrase *Athanasius contra mundum* ("Athanasius against the world") has become almost a cliché, but it is not a bad summary of his position during all the years from his becoming a bishop in 328 until his death in his seventies in 373. He has been called the father of orthodoxy, for through much of his forty-five years as bishop his was almost the only voice raised within the eastern empire on behalf of the traditional teaching of the Church about her Founder. Again and again calumnies were made up about him; on five occasions he was deposed from his episcopal see and exiled. For one period of six or seven years, when his life was threatened, we lose sight of him altogether. It is surmised that he lived those years in the company of his friends the monks in the desert.

The rule of Arianizing emperors and the short-lived attempt of Julian to restore the old paganism were, as we have seen, followed by the reign of the Catholic emperor Theodosius the Great (379-395). Arianism was officially brought to an end within the empire, although its teaching was adopted by some of the barbarian tribes as they adopted the civilization of the regions they conquered. This was still in the future; for the moment the outlook was encouraging. Nevertheless the reign of Theodosius, strong ruler and orthodox Catholic, saw the beginning of three centuries of religious chaos. To deal in detail with all the ecclesiastical quarrels, orthodox and schismatic assemblies of church rulers, and the recurrent interference of secular rulers is beyond the scope of this book. The fact to be kept in mind is not that Catholic emperors interfered on behalf of the Faith and others on the side of Arianism, but that this secular interference came to be accepted as the pattern of things in the eastern empire. The evil that imperial meddling did lived on and its legacy is still to be perceived.

A council meeting in 382 at Constantinople, under the aegis of Theodosius himself, decreed for the see of Constantinople a primacy of honor second only to that of Rome. This had nothing to do with doctrine nor did the first dispute that arose after the innovation. The bishop at the time was St. John surnamed Chrysostom (in Greek "golden-mouthed," on account of his oratory). The bishop of Alexandria at the time was one Theophilus, a worldly, go-getting prelate who envied his colleague the prestige of Constantinople and set to work to supplant him. He did this by means of calumnies which led to St. John's deposition and exile. The popular indignation frightened the intriguers and so the Empress Eudoxia recalled the rightful bishop. A few years later he was again exiled, despite the approval of his work by Pope Innocent I. He died in exile and it was not until his relics were brought back to Constantinople and the emperor had publicly expressed his sorrow that the angry citizens could be appeased.

Two factors chiefly led to all the trouble in the Near East and in the end brought about the schism which still persists. There was, first, the constant striving of the secular power to dominate the Church. This was common to both east and west, but in western Europe the Papacy in the time of barbarian invasion and consequent disorder was the one stable hope of civilization and thus won a position never wholly lost. In the east, secular rulers early seized control and have thereby weakened church authority through the ages. A Byzantine emperor claimed God's warrant for his decisions, seeing himself in some sense priest as well as magistrate.

The second factor to consider is the progressive alienation of east from west in religious matters. This was especially to be seen in 381, when a council called by the emperor met in Constantinople. The fathers were outspoken in confirming the declarations of Nicaea on the divinity of Christ, but in two respects they unwittingly betrayed their position. They made no protest against imperial interference in church government, particularly the appointment of bishops. Secondly, they issued a formal proclamation of their primacy in the east. The supremacy of Rome was not denied, but their jealousy of the See of Peter was obvious and there was no doubt of their contempt for the "barbarism" of the west.

The records of the three centuries after the first Council of Constantinople show the steady encroachment of the secular power on the domain of the Church. In the early part of the fifth century (about 427) Nestorius, bishop of Constantinople, was the center of a new theological dispute. This concerned the union of two natures, divine and human, in the one Person of Jesus Christ. Some earlier heretics had denied the reality of Christ's human nature. Nestorius had another idea. He claimed there were two *persons* in Christ so as to accommodate two *natures*. Nestorius was opposed by St. Cyril, bishop of Alexandria. Both bishops appealed to Rome. The pope approved the teaching of St. Cyril and condemned that of Nestorius. This was clear and unequivocal; Rome had spoken; the matter was settled. The significant point in a long and complicated dispute is that, after Rome's decision, Nestorius appealed to the emperor. The latter, it is true, finally confirmed the Roman decision, but in the meantime both bishops were arrested *after the pontiff had given his judgment*. The saint was upheld and the heretic sent into exile, but the mischief had been done —the recognition of the emperor as the final court of appeal.

3. Let us now look forward about a century and a quarter after the affair of Nestorius. In the middle of the sixth century (547-565) we find ourselves in the empire of Justinian, the famous lawgiver and in some ways the greatest of all the emperors. Another theological dispute was setting Christians, sometimes quite literally, at one another's throats. It had started a century earlier with the teaching of Eutyches, abbot of a monastery in Constantinople. He was an ardent and aggressive monk with a large following. Unfortunately his gifts as a thinker and his knowledge of theology were less than his powers as a leader and a troublemaker. His special theory, based on a distortion of St. Cyril's teaching, was the existence of only one nature in Christ, the divine. The Greek term for this idea gave a name to the heretics, Monophysites, and they are also known, after their leader, as Eutychians. The heresy was still agitating the Church in the east when Justinian became emperor. He sought to settle the dispute

by asking the Monophysite leaders to attend a conference. They refused, so he deposed some of the recalcitrant ones and gave orders for the bishop in office at the time to announce his acceptance of the orthodox belief. Again we see the emperor acting as the final judge in a question of doctrine. Without detracting from the greatness of Justinian as ruler and lawgiver we have to admit that at times he saw the pope as someone to be used by himself, for he felt that on him, the emperor, God had laid the responsibility for the welfare of the Church. The emperor's method was simple and drastic—enforce silence, insist on papal support, and so ensure a tranquil empire. Pope Vigilius was summoned to Constantinople in connection with the theological troubles, and it was seven years before he was allowed to set out for Rome again, dying on the return journey.

Confusion and intrigue followed the death of Justinian I. Another "strong" ruler became emperor, Heraclius, but unfortunately he was won over to the acceptance of the newest heresy. This was monotheletism, which allowed only one source of spiritual activity, one will—the divine one—in Christ. The dispute was complicated and made a future bone of contention for theologians and historians by the vagueness of Pope Honorius I in dealing with the question of a divine and a human will in Christ. Subsequent popes had the task of refuting the errors which Honorius' confusion seemed to support.

In the mid-seventh century a courageous and forthright pope, Martin I, came out bluntly against imperial compromise. The reigning emperor, Constans II, imitating his great predecessor, Justinian, tried the practical politician's device of imposing silence all round and trying to force the pope to back him up. Pope Martin was treated more brutally than Vigilius. His murder was planned, and when that failed he was carried off to Constantinople, tried on trumped-up charges, and sentenced to death.

This was commuted to exile and he was taken to a colonial outpost in the Crimean peninsula. There, worn out by physical and mental sufferings but with an unbroken will, he died.

In the three and a half centuries which followed Constantine's grant of toleration several tendencies which were to shape the form of western civilization had been developing steadily. When Constantinople became the imperial capital, Rome sank to the status of a provincial city, capital of a western empire which the cultured Byzantine Greeks looked on as a barbarous colony. A deputy appointed by the emperor was left to govern it; this exarch, as he was called, made his headquarters in Ravenna, not in Rome. More and more the people of Rome and its environs, thus neglected by the imperial government, came to look on their bishop, whose supremacy was still recognized in east and west, as their earthly ruler as well as their spiritual teacher. Sometimes his relations with the exarch were cordial, sometimes embittered, but to the Romans the distant emperor was always a shadowy and generally an unpopular figure. They looked on their bishop, the Roman pontiff, as the true ruler. He fed them in times of scarcity, dealt with the barbarians of the north, the Lombards, by judicious appeasement at first and by formal treaty when they had been converted. He policed the city, administered justice and, above all, he was their pastor. In Constantinople, contempt was tinged with jealousy. The Patriarch of Constantinople enjoyed great prestige; he was second only to the Bishop of Rome, St. Peter's successor. But why rest content with second place? Not openly at first did any prelate in Constantinople ask this question, but there was a gradually widening breach which would develop into the final chasm between east and west.

The early stages of the rift are shown very clearly in the year 692, when a council convened by the emperor met in his palace to deal with various matters of church discipline. It claimed the authority to legislate for east and west, thereby tacitly regarding the See of Peter as merely one of many episcopates in the empire. Some of the rulings were definitely anti-Roman, such as the disavowal of clerical celibacy. Pope St. Sergius I refused acceptance of these decisions and he might perhaps have shared the fate of Martin I. Happily for him, one of the recurrent upheavals in a decaying empire overthrew the reigning emperor Justinian II, whose rebellious subjects cut off his nose, decreed his exile, and sent him to the Crimea. He regained his throne two years later and opened negotiations with Pope John VII. The latter's diplomatic vagueness was unacceptable to the emperor, but the pope died before he could be cajoled or ordered to go to Constantinople. The next pope patched up the quarrel without accepting the obnoxious decrees, and there the matter stood until the emperor, cruel and rapacious, was assassinated.

In freeing the Church from pagan servitude, Constantine had prepared the way for seeking to submit her to a nominally Christian state. When he shifted the imperial capital to the east, the Church in that area began to suffer more than in the west from the conflict between the claims of God and Caesar. Unhappily, what one can only label the snobbery of Byzantine rulers towards the west was shared by many of the eastern churchmen. The Roman pontiff's supremacy was still recognized in theory, but eastern jealousy grew and there was often friction.

Within about a century and a half of the dispute between the emperor and Pope Martin I occurred the Photian schism, when an able, ambitious politician-turned-ecclesiastic quarreled with the canonically appointed bishop in Constantinople and supplanted him. Photius (about 820-891) had been a military officer and then a civil servant. In order to become patriarch he received all the canonical orders up to and including episcopal ones within six days. Later he was deposed and exiled, but the rift had grown to something like a chasm. The mischief continued intermittently until the complete break in the eleventh century. There were, it is true, theological differences between Rome and some of the eastern churchmen. The dispute about the *filioque* clause in the Creed, concerning the relationship between the three Persons of the Holy Trinity, was the outstanding quarrel. It was the most important of all at the time because it dealt with a matter of Christian dogma. We may wonder, however, whether even this would have wrenched the eastern hierarchy away from Roman unity had Byzantine prelates been as zealous in the service of God as of the emperor. That, of course, is one of the might-have-beens of history. We are left with the hope that the chasm can yet be bridged and that a great Uniate Church may once again be united to her Roman and Latin sister.

3. The Church of the Fathers and the Monks

1. A believing Christian and still more one who accepts the authority of the Catholic and Roman Church reads with sorrow of the cleavage between east and west that began when Constantine left Rome and set up his new capital on the Bosphorus. Quarrels arose, generally with imperial support for eastern prelates, and schisms took place, partly because of theological disputes but often for political reasons. They were adjusted, but broke out later over new differences. Finally the rupture took place which still exists, leaving in schism millions of eastern Christians who share Rome's orders, sacraments, many of her devotions, and most of her doctrines. The majority of these separated brethren now live under governments hostile to all supernatural belief.

Before any lasting break occurred, two great developments of Christian life made their appearance. We may call them the emergence of the Christian intellectuals and the rise of Christian monks. The terms are not mutually exclusive. When a civilization based on Christian belief had reached its zenith in the Middle Ages the intellectuals were generally in the ranks of the monks and their somewhat later brethren the friars.*

The primitive Church lived in obscurity, persecuted, ostracized, and despised by educated pagans. As soon, however, as she obtained her freedom she began the propaganda of the written word, which indeed we may even trace back to the letters of St. Paul to his various groups of converts.

The earliest of the Church's intellectuals, when we have passed the apostolic age, were the writers we call the apologists. They wrote for their still-pagan fellow countrymen. Often they themselves were adult converts to Christianity and were eager to show that the religion they had embraced was morally good and was not irrational. There was sometimes the additional motive of seeking to avert persecution of the Christians, for some of the apologias were addressed to the emperors.

In the east the apologetic writers were in contact with the subtle, speculative Greek mind, sometimes rationalistic, sometimes mystical as well, as in the case of the Alexandrian Platonists. Western apologists generally had a more realistic, down-to-earth mentality, that of the Romans, whose pagan religion was a department of the state bureaucracy. Asked to pick an outstanding eastern representative of this school of writing, one would almost certainly choose Titus Flavius Clemens, known to posterity as St. Clement of Alexandria. He was born a pagan Greek, about 150 A.D., but spent most of his life after his conversion teaching and writing in the Egyptian city that was one of the cultural centers of the world. We know little

* Monks and friars, both living the religious life and bound by vows, differ, nominally anyhow, in their objectives. The monk is called to a cloistered life of prayer, penance, and study. The friar adds to these obligations active missionary labors outside his cloister. Thus the Trappists and the Carthusians are monks, the Franciscans, Dominicans, and Carmelites friars. In practice, monks in all eras, including our own, have often been called upon for active work when the Church needed their aid.

about his personality, except that he seems to have been a winning and lovable priest whose written and spoken words made many converts among the Greek intellectuals. In depth of thought and bold speculation he was outstripped by his pupil Origen.

With the latter we have left the early apologists and are dealing with the great constructive thinkers we call the Fathers of the Church. In spite of his ascetic life and the fact that he died as a confessor of the Faith as a result of his sufferings in the Decian persecution, Origen (died about 254 A.D.) has lain under a shadow in church history. There is the deplorable incident of his self-mutilation through a too-literal application of Christ's saying about those who make themselves eunuchs for the kingdom of heaven. More serious is the suspicion of unorthodox ideas which led to some of his writings being condemned.

After Origen's death the Church in the east had a galaxy of brilliant writers whom we call the Greek Fathers. We have already seen St. Athanasius, bishop of Alexandria, standing alone against an Arian hierarchy and government in defense of the true doctrine of the Incarnation. His moral and physical courage would of themselves suffice for his reputation to live, but besides that he was a deep thinker and a great writer. He is what St. Bernard called a *vir ecclesiae* (a man of the Church), one of the outstanding churchmen of history. We shall meet him again in the early phase of Christian monasticism.

Eminent for learning and sanctity is the group of three bishops we call the Cappadocian Fathers, from the name of their native province in the eastern part of Asia Minor. All three stand out as theologians and writers and as defenders of sound doctrine against Arianism. The three Fathers are St. Basil the Great (about 330-379), his younger brother St. Gregory of Nyssa (about 331-396), and the friend of both of them, St. Gregory Nazianzen (about 339-396). All three, the two brothers and the friend, were united by a deep affection which brightens and warms the story of their lives as pastors and writers and of their contests and hardships in the fight for orthodox teaching. By the standards of outward achievement the elder brother, Basil, who was bishop of Caesarea, stands out in this trio for his work as writer and skilled administrator. Moreover, he was a prelate of much personal charm, with a tender and cheerful nature that prompts comparison with St. Philip Neri as portrayed by Newman —a "saint of gentleness and kindness." St. Basil, like St. Athanasius, was closely connected with the monastic movement. These three bishops were influenced in their student days by the Christianized Platonic thought of St. Clement of Alexandria and his pupil Origen, both given to speculation and to seeking mystical allegories in the text of the Bible.

In contrast to these three, but at one with them in personal goodness, is St. John Chrysostom, the bishop of Constantinople, whose life (345-407) ended in exile brought about by the intrigues of his enemies. The Chrysostom of his name perpetuates his reputation as a preacher, but we know him also as a philanthropist, whose income was largely spent on hospitals and other good works in his see. As a theologian and Biblical scholar he stands for the Antioch school, textual, realistic, and literal as contrasted with the allegorical exegesis of the Alexandrians.

The last of the famous Greek Fathers, for he died in the middle of the eighth century, is St. John Damascene (or "of Damascus"), theologian and hymn writer. He is a link with the Catholic intellectualism of the Middle Ages, for he is the first great Christian writer influenced by Aristotle's philosophy. Like St. John Chrysostom, he was an eloquent preacher, but posterity knows him chiefly for his defense of sacred images as an aid to devotion against the fanaticism of the Iconoclasts or image breakers.

In the great Greek Fathers we find the subtlety as well

as the clarity of Greek thought baptized into Christianity and fused with the monotheism and the ethics of Judaism. During the best period of pagan Rome, the late Republic, and the early Empire, Greek thought had been assimilated and adapted to Roman ways of thinking by such writers as Cicero, in his nonpolitical works, and Seneca. A similar task of adaptation on Christian lines was then carried out by the Latin Fathers. This movement had its roots not, as we might expect, in Rome itself or even in Italy, but in North Africa. What had once been the Carthaginian Empire and is now predominantly a Moslem area full of unrest and violence was in the early Christian centuries a flourishing and highly developed section of the Roman Empire.

2.   The Church in North Africa has a wonderful record of martyrs, apologists, and theologians, closed by the greatest name of all, that of St. Augustine of Hippo, as the waves of barbarism were swamping a whole civilization. In some ways it is a unique chapter in history. Christian idealism and virtuous living are seen side by side with every kind of moral corruption, public and private. In the Christian writers of the time we see the ardor and emotionalism of the African races. The Roman mind was free of racial and color prejudices, and so the qualities of colonial peoples were often wedded to the Roman sense of order and discipline. In these early African Christians we are conscious of the African fervor and ebullience contending with the seriousness, the *gravitas,* which was part of the Roman ideal.

Nearly contemporary with St. Clement of Alexanderia was the Tertullian of whom we have spoken. In genius he was the equal of St. Clement of Alexandria and perhaps even of the brilliant Origen, but in temperament very different. The two Alexandrians were gentle, tolerant, mystical; Tertullian was fiercely intolerant of the pagan culture in which he had been brought up, and he was an intellectual scornful of mere intellect. He was a master of invective, scourging abuses, doctrinal or moral, in his vigorous Latin. His *Apologeticus* is one of the classical defenses of Christian belief. In the later years of his long life his excessive fervor led him astray and he joined the rigoristic Montanists. It was a sad loss for the Church he had served so long. We remain in his debt for a vocabulary that has served theology well through the ages.

Born a decade or so later than Tertullian, whom he regarded as teacher and exemplar, and surviving him by more then three decades is St. Cyprian, bishop of Carthage. Scion of a pagan family and, like many well-born young men of the Empire, trained in rhetoric and law, he became a Christian in his forties. Two years after his baptism he was made bishop of Carthage by popular election. If we seek records of personal traits we shall find that he was an enthusiastic convert, with zeal equal to that of his master Tertullian, but saved by an inner discipline and humility from his master's arrogance. Cyprian, inheriting a good deal of wealth, was notably generous to the poor. What we know of his life in Carthage suggests a division of his time and energy between intellectual labors, philanthropy, and pastoral duties. In the end he died a martyr's death. He was beheaded in 258 A.D., the first African martyr-bishop. Of his writings the most important for later generations has been the *De Unitate Catholicae Ecclesiae* ("Of the Unity of the Catholic Church"), for here, in a book written in Africa in the middle of the third century, is a clear exposition of the *Roman* Catholic claims—of a Church founded on Peter and entrusted by Christ to Peter and his successors.

Three lesser names, not of "Fathers of the Church" but of apologists and controversialists in the early Christian centuries, demand mention even in a brief story of the Church, Minucius Felix, Arnobius, and Lactantius. All three, the first a Roman, the other two Africans, were highly educated men of upper-class families, and they emphasize the appeal of the Faith to the intellectuals of their time. They attack the gibe, of their own and later times, that Christianity was a religion of slaves and illiterates. The three are interesting as showing the Church in the west already in possession of the language and the thought of the best Latin culture. Minucius was an elderly convert lawyer who wrote a dialogue (*Octavius*) between a Christian and a pagan to refute popular errors about the Christian religion. Arnobius, like St. Paul before him, was a one-time enemy converted to the Faith he had attacked. He wrote his *Adversus Gentes* as a pamphlet against the old pagan religion. His chief claim on posterity, however, is that one of his pupils was Lactantius, the third of our trio, known as the Christian Cicero. He was beloved of our medieval ancestors, less for his polemical writings than for a book *De Mortibus Persecutorum*, telling grisly stories of the deaths of some of the anti-Christian emperors. In his later years Minucius settled in Europe as tutor to Crispus, son of the emperor Constantine.

Near the end of the patristic age, or era of the Fathers of the Church, we meet the four greatest of the Latin Fathers. They are Saints Ambrose, Jerome, Augustine, and Gregory (first pope of that name), whom the men of the Middle Ages held in only slightly less esteem than the four Evangelists. Starting with the birth of St. Ambrose, before the middle of the fourth century, and ending with the death of Pope St. Gregory the Great in 604 A.D., their lives span two and a half centuries between the early Church and the chaotic period we call the Dark Ages.

The first of these Fathers, St. Ambrose (about 339-397), bishop of Milan, is known to the general reader chiefly as the mentor and spiritual father of St. Augustine of Hippo. He was more than the instrumental cause of bringing a wayward pagan genius into the Christian fold. Ambrose stands alongside such men as Hildebrand (Pope St. Gregory VII), St. Thomas of Canterbury, and Pope Innocent III as one of the great churchmen of history. Trained to law and administration and the holder of high offices in the state before his conversion, he showed himself a wise ruler of his great see, a fearless fighter against worldliness and heresy, an eloquent preacher and hymnologist,* reformer of church music and a tireless writer on theology and Biblical interpretation. Lastly, he was ascetic and saint. St. Ambrose insisted on the supremacy of the Church in spiritual things. The emperor, he said, was within the Church and, as a Christian, subject to its authority, not above it.

Contemporary with St. Ambrose but outliving him by about twenty years was St. Jerome (about 347-419). He was born in a well-to-do provincial family who were orthodox Catholics, and he was educated in the best Roman tradition. In early life he read widely in Latin and Greek and later on added Hebrew to his accomplishments. Augustine was a deeper thinker, Ambrose a more experienced administrator, but Jerome was the most erudite of the Latin Fathers. His life was that of a scholar and largely a recluse; for six years he lived as a hermit in the Syrian desert. The painters have familiarized us with the picture of him in his library in Bethlehem amid his books and manuscripts and with his symbolical lion near him. Like Origen, whose writings he admired, he was steeped in the text of the Bible. It is above all as the translator of the Bible into the living Latin of his period that he has been so great a force in the Church; the "lion Latin" of Jerome's Vulgate is the authentic voice of Roman Christianity. Those who have enough Latinity to read them may enjoy

* To him the Church owes some of her most beautiful hymns, such as *Aeterne rerum Conditor* and *Deus Creator omnium,* but the charming story of St. Ambrose and St. Augustine together composing alternate stanzas of the *Te Deum* at the latter's baptism seems to be without foundation.

his letters. He was a very human saint as one meets him in the letters. He could be friendly and solicitous in giving spiritual direction to the pious Eustochium and other devout women who had him for a director, but in controversy he was often irritable and choleric, perhaps because of a digestion ruined by excessive fasting in his earlier asceticism. Above all things, St. Jerome is the father of Biblical scholarship.

Six or seven years after St. Jerome was born, an earnest Christian woman married to a pagan civil servant gave birth to a male child in the African province of Numidia. The child was named, but not baptized, Aurelius Augustinus; the official registration of the birth names the father as Patricius, a magistrate of the town of Tagaste, and the mother as Monnica (popularly but less correctly Monica). Was the infant purely Roman by descent, as was once believed, or partly Berber? We do not know, nor is it important, but a touch of African blood might explain some features of his passionate temperament. Anyhow, it suffices for posterity that on a November day in 354 A.D. was born a child who was to become the greatest of the Latin Fathers and Doctors of the Church and one of the chief intellectual forces in the new western civilization that would arise on the ruins of the Roman Empire.

His mother's solicitude did not keep the young Augustine on the straight path of her own virtuous living as he grew into adolescence and manhood. Madaura, where he went to school, and Carthage, where he started his higher studies, offered only too much opportunity for the average sensual man who wished to sow his wild oats. That story and the record of his delvings into many religions and philosophies form the subject matter of the earlier part of the book of his *Confessions*. Then came the departure to Milan to study rhetoric, and his conversion, largely brought about by the preaching of St. Ambrose.

St. Augustine has left us the greatest of all spiritual autobiographies.

Anyone trying to summarize briefly Augustine's intellectual quality and his achievement as thinker and writer may be forgiven if he is both puzzled and desperate. Jerome, as we remarked, was more learned, Tertullian at least as well skilled in controversy, and other Latin writers of the period could compete with Augustine as stylists. When all is said, he towers above all the Christian intellectuals of the western world. In one respect at least this preeminence is explicable. The Christian Church was born of Judaism, which had rejected the promised Messiah when He came. St. Paul, an educated Hellenistic Jew as well as a mystic, brought to the infant Church the mental pattern of that Hebraic-Greek background. So things were for three centuries. The educated Christians were dominated by the Greek genius when they applied their intellects to the truths of the Faith. Even Tertullian, master of Christian paradox in the Latin idiom, did not break away from the domination of Athens and Alexandria grafted on to the spirit of Israel. Then came Augustine, and after that the supremacy of Athens and Alexandria was at an end. That, perhaps, is as near as one may come to expressing briefly the revolutionary effect of this Father on western thought. He achieved his result by means of a tremendous body of writing—treatises on the Unity and Trinity of God, on human nature and divine grace, freedom of the will and divine foreknowledge, and the monument of historical writing in *The City of God.*

The *Confessions* will always remain the best loved of Augustine's writings. After fifteen centuries its writer's passionate African nature, his depth of affection, gift for friendship, mental curiosity and, finally, his absorption, emotional and intellectual, in the contemplation of God, make his autobiography an unforgettable book. One of his sayings sums up all the aspiration of a lifetime: *Fecisti nos ad Te, Domine, et inquietum est cor nostrum donec requiescat in Te* ("Thou hast made us for Thyself, O Lord, and our heart is uneasy until it rest in Thee").

As a champion of orthodox belief, St. Augustine lives in history as the opponent of Donatism and Pelagianism. Donatus, who gave his name to the first of these heresies, held that the bishops and other clergy who had weakened under persecution and denied the Faith thereby lost their priestly powers—a teaching that would make chaos of all sacramental acts, for who is to judge other men's souls as known to the mind of God? Pelagius (360-420) was a British monk whose ideas anticipate the typically British Victorian attitude of "self help" and "progress." Man, said Pelagius, was not truly a "fallen" being; his own efforts would suffice for his winning salvation. One can see why St. Augustine stressed the Fall of Man and why he is above all the "Doctor of Grace."

St. Augustine died (430 A.D.) as the Vandals were besieging his diocesan town of Hippo. By that time the process we know as the fall of the Roman Empire was steadily eroding the "one world" of the Republic and the emperors. Nevertheless we should qualify our idea of that fall. It was not everywhere or all the time merely violence, ruin, and chaos. The barbarians were not always wholly barbarous, and although they destroyed much they also assimilated much. Many of them were already Christians of a sort, Arians or semi-Arians, when they invaded or infiltrated the imperial territories. Some of them renounced Arianism and became orthodox; others passed directly from paganism to Catholicism.

The process of mingled destruction and renewal was over by the time the fourth of the great Latin Fathers, Pope St. Gregory I, was born (about 540 A.D.) The disappearance of the *Pax Romana,* the peace under law of the Roman Empire, might have left a vacuum fatal to western civilization had it not been for the Catholic Church. She took over the language, the modes of thought, and much of the organization of the Empire and laid the foundations of medieval Christendom. Great leaders arose to direct this movement, the greatest of them St. Gregory I. He became pope—unwillingly—when he was about fifty years old and ruled the Church for the next fourteen years until his death in 604.

Gregory was not an erudite scholar like Jerome nor a deep, original thinker like Augustine, nor had he the classical culture and the vein of poetry of St. Ambrose, but he shared with the great bishop of Milan a genius for administration. Merely to list some of the things he did for the Church is to outline a vast achievement carried out in less than a decade and a half on the papal throne. He reformed clerical life, organized and fostered a form of monasticism suited to the western world, set afoot great missionary enterprises, and left behind him a large body of pastoral and devotional writing. Above all, he built up on solid foundations the authority and prestige of the Papacy. Thereby he gave the impetus to a movement that would be all to the good in the turbulent centuries after his death.

Despite this strenuous life's work, Gregory, born into an aristocratic and wealthy family, had no more earnest desire than to live as a simple monk. Only one ambition for work outside his monastery possessed him, namely, to carry Christianity to the pagan Anglo-Saxons in their marshy, thickly wooded island in the northern sea. They had caught his imagination, according to the tradition, when he saw in the Roman slave market some Anglo-Saxon boys for sale. Gregory was a man of a sunny and genial disposition and the story of his punning comments

on the *Angli* and *angeli* ("Angles and angels") and on
God's wrath and the Anglo-Saxon kingdom of Deira (*Dei
ira* and Deira) is quite in character.

3. While the organization of the Church was being developed and her statements of fundamental doctrines receiving their final form even before the persecutions were
over, another movement was beginning. At first it was a
matter of individual religious life, not centralized and
with only a minimum of organization. We call it monasticism. It has an unbroken history from, at latest, the middle of the third century to our own time. It has had many
ups and downs and given birth to many different institutions, but in essence it has been the same throughout the
centuries. We can sum up its nature by saying that it consists in carrying out Christ's counsel to the young man
who sought perfection: "Sell all that thou hast and give
to the poor and come follow Me." In the language of
theologians, it is adding the counsels of perfection to the
commandments binding on all Christians.

The form which the movement took at first is implied
in the name given it. "Monasticism" is derived from the
Greek adjective μόνος ("alone"). The first Christians to
lead the monastic life—we find a similar practice in some
non-Christian systems—were men and, later, women, who
fled from human society to devote themselves entirely to
the worship of God and to progress in the spiritual life.
The traditional founder of Christian monasticism is St.
Paul of Thebes, a hermit of whom we know very little except his sanctity, his longevity, and his friendship with a
certain Anthony, an Egyptian Christian born about 250
A.D. Of Anthony we know little more than about Paul,
for the only source material is a brief "Life" by St.
Athanasius, who was an admirer and promoter of monasticism when he was bishop of Alexandria. His *Vita An-
tonii* was written for devotional reading or "edification"

and lacks the personal touches we have come to look for in biography. Anthony was born into peasant-farmer society in the valley of the Nile some sixty miles below Cairo. He had only the rudiments of an education. He inherited the family property when he and a young sister were the last surviving members. He placed the girl with some pious spinsters leading a devout life in common. They had probably made vows of chastity under episcopal supervision. This dedication to celibacy by *continentes* as they were called was an early practice which antedates any kind of formal monasticism. Anthony sold or gave away most of the patrimony and retired to the desert, first in Egypt, then in Syria and for a time in Arabia. Sometimes his dwelling was a wattle-and-mud hut, at one period an empty tomb shared with small mammals and reptiles, later an abandoned fort, also shared with the local fauna. Modern readers are little impressed by details which St. Athanasius thought would edify his readers, such as the fact that the saint's austerities included a lifelong abstention from washing. Flaubert and others have fictionalized the famous "temptations," without much regard for the few recorded facts.

Anthony sought only solitude and silence for himself, but involuntarily he had started a "movement." He became a beloved master and had to accept disciples. Many Egyptians as well as Greeks living in Egypt built themselves hermitages in the desert, some of them near the saint's own dwelling. He could not avoid being father and guide to these neophytes. He made several trips to Alexandria and in his own fashion helped his friend the bishop in the fight against Arianism. Once he arrived in the midst of a persecution of orthodox believers and seems to have sought martyrdom, but the local ruler, whether from humanity or prudence, took no action beyond checking the work of the anchorites among the prisoners awaiting trial or execution.

As leadership and authority were the last things Anthony desired, it was left to another to organize and consolidate the work of monasticism. This was done by St. Pachomius, who founded a large monastery at Tabennisi some time before the middle of the fourth century. Pachomius had been a soldier in Constantine's army before his conversion. He had a convert's zeal and a soldier's love of order and discipline. The earlier ascetics had been *monks* in the strict sense, that is, solitaries. They were individualists who adopted the practices of a veteran ascetic of their choice or embarked on a regimen of their own. Hence the variety of original and even freakish practices we read about—fasts carried to the limit of human endurance, sleep restricted to uneasy cat naps in the midst of basket weaving or, as in the case of St. Simeon Stylites, years passed on top of a ruined column. The reader of the *Vitae Patrum* ("Lives of the Fathers of the Desert") is aware at times of a motive of record breaking in the ascetic practices.

We come suddenly on the religious life as lived in the modern Church when we read the *Rule* of St. Basil the Great (about 330-379), bishop of Caesarea from 370 until his death. In his early manhood he had studied the hermit life of Syria and Egypt and had traveled about the Near East in order to meet many of the ascetics. His own *Rule,* still followed by Basilian houses under Roman obedience as well as by monks of the Eastern Orthodox Church,* softens the military spirit of Pachomius with a

---

* The Eastern Orthodox Church, nominally subject to its ecumenical patriarch, consists of a number of virtually independent churches, for example, in the U.S.S.R., Greece, Rumania. They are, unhappily, not in union with Rome, but have a valid priesthood and valid sacraments. The term "Greek Catholic Church," sometimes used for the Orthodox Church, is inaccurate. There are, however, various bodies of authentic Catholics whose use of non-Latin languages—Greek, Old Slavonic, Syriac —and various traditional practices not seen in Roman Catholic churches, is permitted by Rome. Such, for instance, are the Maronites and Melchites,

gentleness that was a trait of this bishop, who combined a quick temper and a gift for command with much sweetness of disposition. The *Rule* of St. Basil is the true link between the early, solitary monasticism of the Near East —Egypt, Syria, and Palestine—and the cenobitical, that is, community, life of western monasteries. A form of monastic life akin to the earlier type, with solitude, silence, and great austerity, arose in Ireland when the country was bloodlessly and rapidly Christianized in the fifth century.

4. The great name in western monasticism is that of St. Benedict of Nursia, but we find his kind of community life anticipated by a Gallic churchman. St. Martin, afterwards bishop of Tours, whom we see as a soldier on horseback dividing his cloak with his sword so as to share it with a beggar—before the soldier was a baptized Christian—established a monastery near Poitiers as early as the latter part of the fourth century. Then came St. Honoratus, who died (429 A.D.) about half a century before the birth of St. Benedict. St. Honoratus' monastery was on the island of Lerins, off the coast of southern France. In common with the Irish monasteries and the later Benedictine houses it became famous as a center of learning. Like the Irish monasteries it helped to preserve Europe's classical heritage when successive waves of barbarism threatened to sweep it all away. Lerins stands midway between the hermit life of the desert and the milder form of later monasticism.

St. Gregory is our earliest informant about St. Benedict, the patriarch of western monks, who was born about 480 in an aristocratic family in central Italy. He was sent to the best Roman schools. Shocked by the licentious life around him, he fled from Rome; he was, perhaps, older at

---

both with flourishing parishes in the U.S.A. Some eight million Catholics, loyal to the Holy See, are members of the non-Latin groups in the Church.

the time than St. Gregory's account suggests. Benedict lived in a cave at Subiaco, about forty miles from the city. He was formally inducted as a monk by a friend in a nearby religious house. The young hermit's light could not be hidden under a bushel, and he was elected abbot of an Umbrian monastery. His zeal for reform was too much for some of his subjects, and they drove him away after an attempt to poison him. Halfway to Naples he climbed a mountain, Monte Cassino, and found another cave. He overturned and destroyed a heathen image, gathered a few companions together, converted the local country people in Cassinum, and thus laid the foundation of one of the greatest monastic centers in the western world. The monastery on Monte Cassino was a nursery for saints and scholars for more than fifteen centuries. The school's most famous pupil was St. Thomas Aquinas.

Again and again the monastery has been destroyed, the last time by Allied bombs and artillery fire in the second world war. The monks have once more, with infinite patience, rebuilt their home on the devastated site.

St. Benedict's instructions for his monks are contained in the *Holy Rule* which he compiled in his middle age, after some thirty years as a simple monk and then as a religious superior. St. Gregory cites "discretion" as the conspicuous feature of the rule; we may regard the word as a synonym for "moderation." St. Benedict did not ask his monks to live in unbroken silence or to endure the extreme physical austerity of the desert solitaries. Scholarship, as well as asceticism, entered into the scheme, and for everybody, choir monk as well as lay coadjutor, work of some kind or other was compulsory. Work *is* prayer, said the saint: *Laborare est orare* ("To labor is to pray"). Decorous and fervent worship in choir, he calls the *Opus Dei* ("Work of God"); through the ages his monks have held a leading place as exemplars and propagators of liturgical worship according to the Roman rite.

With St. Benedict and his biographer St. Gregory the Great we are on the threshold of a new age, that of the growth of medieval Christendom. We now must return in imagination to the period following Constantine's edict which ended the persecutions, for in those centuries the Church was, above all else, busied in the task that Christ had committed to her: "Go ye and teach all nations." Christian belief and practice were to fill the place left by a dying paganism.

4. The Church of the Early Missionaries

1. From her earliest days the Church was conscious of her duty to make converts. The first Christians were Jewish and it needed St. Peter's vision (Acts 10:9-17) and the driving force of St. Paul's enthusiasm to start the worldwide missionary effort which has gone on from the first Pentecost to the days of the Iron Curtain and Red China.

When Constantine gave Christian believers religious and civic freedom in 313, there was an upsurge of church activity such as works of charity, the building of places of worship, the development of liturgical services, and the acquisition of property for church purposes. The emperor himself was especially generous in restoring sequestrated property and in giving money or land for building. Most important of all was the evangelization of pagan society, now made possible on a larger scale. Even when persecution was raging, this work was carried on. By the end of the third century a large part, estimated by Adolf von Harnack, the German historian, as about a half, of the empire's population had become Christian. Only on the frontiers in the Near East and the north were there few or no Christians. Most of northwestern Italy, the interior of Gaul, and all Germany were still pagan. Around the Black Sea and eastwards, Christianity was unknown.

After the end of the third century, missionary enterprise reached all the borders of the Roman Empire. By the year 300 the Faith had been carried to Armenia by St. Gregory the Illuminator, the first *catholicos* or metropolitan in that region. Much is uncertain in the records of this bishop, and it may be that the ground had been prepared for his work by Syrian missionaries. The historians unite in giving him credit for one thing—his staunch fidelity to the full doctrine of the Incarnation; he sent a delegate to support the declarations of the Council of Nicaea in 325. After a career of labor and hardship, starting, so we are told, in his youth with a fourteen-year imprisonment in a pit for his religion, he resigned his position and spent his last years as a hermit.

It was not until the middle of the ninth century that the Christian religion was carried to the Slavs and the Tatars in what is now European Russia. This was the work of two remarkable men, probably of Slavic descent but Hellenized by their family's residence in Thessalonica. St. Methodius, the "Apostle of the Slavs," and his younger brother St. Cyril had given up wealth and social position to become monks and, later, missionaries. Besides doing much work in central and southeastern Europe and enduring injustice from jealous clerics, they gave their Russian converts a Slavonic liturgy* and won papal approval for it in spite of opposition and intrigue.

Earlier than the Christianization of the Slavs was the conversion of the Goths and Visigoths in central Europe by the bishop and scholar Ulfilas. He produced a Gothic version of the Bible and has been called the father of Teutonic literature. Unhappily his name is under a cloud. As

---

* From the Greek λειτουργία meaning, literally public work (that is, worship). The word is more correctly applied—always in the Eastern Church—to the Eucharistic service.

a young *lector,* a cleric in minor orders, in Constantinople he imbibed Arian ideas. Later he seems to have taken a more moderate position as a semi-Arian, but we do not know how far he went away from or back to orthodoxy. The religious welfare of the Goths was in St. John Chrysostom's mind, for he founded a seminary or college to train missionaries for them in Constantinople in 398.

The conversion of the northern islands is shrouded in uncertainty. St. Anshar or Angsgar, who lived through the first half of the ninth century, preached to the Vikings; the kings Haakon "the Good" and Olaf Tryggvason attempted, without much success, to Christianize Norway and some of the northern islands. It was a long time before the whole population of eastern and northeastern Europe was converted to Christianity.

The Near East and the Mediterranean littoral were almost wholly Christian long before central and northern Europe had ceased to be pagan and largely barbarian. We must bear in mind that by the time missionaries were at work on the frontiers of the empire the imperial fabric was already crumbling. The well-made roads and post stations were falling into decay, laws and treaties were being flouted, and from the border provinces such as Britain, with its defensive wall against northern barbarians, garrisons were called home to defend the shrinking frontiers. It is no wonder that St. Augustine of Hippo, dying while the Vandals were fighting their way into his city, and Pope St. Gregory I, two centuries later, harassed by years of Lombard forays, believed the end of the world was near and welcomed the prospect. We should contemplate Europe in the period between the reign of Constantine and the revival of civilization, which rose to a high level in the twelfth century and reached its apex in the thirteenth, when we think of the early missionaries. With the picture of that crumbling empire in mind we

tan guess at the intrepid character of the men who set out
to carry the Christian religion to the heathen.

2. The conversion of the western fringe of what was
then the known world is a story of high sanctity and almost incredible achievement. Two main signposts guide
the reader through the complex record of the centuries
between the ancients and our modern world.

The first fact claiming our attention is that every one
of the missionaries who evangelized the west was formed
by monasticism. Whatever the critic may say of the desert
fathers, he cannot brand the western missionary monks as
escapists. The early monasteries were normally oases of
peace, prayerful and scholarly, in a wilderness of violence,
fraud, rapacity, and lust. It is not much of an exaggeration to say that in the period before the early medieval
renaissance Europe was largely ruled by gangsters. The
genuinely "great" men of that time were nearly all monks.
The "strong" men, the barons, counts, and so forth, do
not even occupy footnotes in the history books, but the
names of Martin of Tours, Patrick, Augustine of Canterbury, Wilfrid, and Boniface are household words all over
the western world.

The second thing to note is the relation between Irish
and British missionary work. We may describe it as a kind
of spiritual exchange between Britain and the western island. Britain gave Ireland the Faith through the labors
of the British-born, French-trained monk Patricius, St.
Patrick; Ireland repaid the debt in good measure by sending missionaries across the Irish Sea, first of all to her
Celtic cousins in Britain and later to those who suppressed
and supplanted them, the Anglo-Saxons.

Most saints have been wronged by legend makers and
hagiographers. Of few of them is this more true than St.
Patrick. We know only too little of that good and admira-

ble bishop, but that little suffices to strip his name of the childish and sometimes dishonoring myths of the romancers and the vulgarization of St. Patrick's Day rhetoric.* Patrick was of good British stock in the west or northwest of what is now England, speaking the old Celtic tongue of the country but born into Roman citizenship and the amenities of Romanized British life. He was captured and carried into slavery in his boyhood or early youth by a raiding party from across the Irish Sea and thereafter spent some unhappy years working as shepherd and farm hand in northern Ireland. After six years of servitude he escaped, made his way to the coast, persuaded a pagan sea captain to take him to France—a series of happenings certainly providential, regarded as miraculous by the chroniclers—and received his education in one of the great monasteries. Some writers think he was at Auxerre under St. Germanus, who was both abbot and bishop. Other accounts place him in St. Honoratus' monastery on the island of Lerins. In either case the long monastic sojourn, twenty to thirty years, mentioned by some histories is improbable. A man of Patrick's ability would have become very learned in all that time in such a place, but he was never a great scholar. He had mastered the Irish form of the Celtic language while in slavery, but his Latin was always poor and, as shown in the *Confessio,* one of his few extant writings known to be genuine, he was not a deeply learned philosopher or theologian. His academic shortcomings do not dim his reputation. His great achievement was the conversion of virtually the whole Irish people.

There are doubtful traces of earlier missionary efforts, perhaps by missionaries from Roman—and Christian—Britain, but Patrick, after his studies and ordination, fol-

* One of the finest jobs of rehabilitation of a noble name in our time is Paul Gallico's *The Steadfast Man; a Biography of St. Patrick,* New York, 1958.

lowed by episcopal consecration, sailed for what was then a pagan country. For him its memories were of slavery—loneliness, homesickness, bodily and mental suffering. Only a great sense of vocation gave him strength to leave his friends the Gallic monks, say farewell to the peaceful life of the cloister, and set out for Ireland. We know what he did there—spread the Faith, built churches, trained a native clergy to serve them, founded schools and monasteries, set the beautiful high-born woman Brigit on the road to sanctity as part nun, part lay preacher, and then died about the middle of the fifth century, still an exile, still homesick but thanking God for all that had been done.

Together with the Christian religion, Patrick had given monasticism to the Irish as he had learned it in France. In the ardent Irish temperament there was a vein of spiritual Quixotry. They yearned to do things the hard way, to accomplish the almost impossible, so they developed a monastic life akin to that of the desert fathers. Later on they modified their rules and adopted something more like the Benedictinism of Europe, but to this day the monastic rule that is most characteristic of the country is the strict Cistercian form, that of the Trappists. In one important respect the Irish monks did not copy the ascetics of the Egyptian desert. They did not despise books and learning or contemn natural beauty and the arts. European civilization is in their debt; they, like their monastic brethren overseas, saved much that was in danger of perishing from the earth. They were pioneers in the making of beautiful books, and from their *scriptoria* or writing rooms came some of the best of early penmanship and illumination.

The Celtic monks of the sixth and seventh centuries stand out, above all, for their missionary zeal. The Celtic Church in Wales and Scotland presumably had its origin in the Roman Christianity of the imperial province of

Britannia, but it departed from Roman practice in various minor details such as the date of Easter, the monastic tonsure, some liturgical customs. The Church in Ireland was, humanly speaking, St. Patrick's creation. Now, while the Celtic believers who survived on the British mainland had nearly everything in common with their Irish brethren, the Irish had an advantage over the British in one respect. This was that the occasion had not yet arisen (the Danish invasion) for them to have embittered memories of Nordic aggression to live down as had the Britons. Christian Britain had never been allowed armaments and native forces by her Roman masters and so was left defenseless when the Roman garrisons were withdrawn. Thus the eastern coastline of a rich, cultivated, and highly civilized country was left accessible to the shallow-draft vessels of the raiders from across the North Sea—Vikings, Angles, Saxons, Danes, Frisians. Murder, torture, rapine, arson, and enslavement leave indelible memories. Why, asked the monks and priests of Wales and Scotland, should they go forth to preach to the savages who had seized or had laid waste the fertile southern and eastern regions of the land of which the Christian owners had been dispossessed? This understandable feeling survived to breed jealousy and distrust when the Anglo-Saxons had been converted and had their own clergy.

Before and during the years when the missionary monks sent to England by Pope St. Gregory I were at work among the pagan peoples settled in the land, the Irish monks were engaged in the same heroic task. Their chosen field was the northern part of the former Roman colony of *Anglia,* the Anglo-Saxon province of Northumbria and parts of eastern Scotland. Their method conformed to the general pattern of monastic missions in those days. A small party went as advance guard into pagan territory, ready for martyrdom if need be. More often, however, they made friends and won the confidence of the pagans by their virtues and by the useful arts they taught the people. The wattle-and-clay shacks of the barbarians were replaced by buildings of stone and timber, the latter especially in the thickly forested parts of England, and soon a monastic settlement would become a center of Christian life and industry. Generally the local abbot would also become the bishop, ruling the Anglo-Saxon laity as well as his monastic subjects.

Something of this kind was the origin of the famous monastic settlement on Iona, whose name is simply a corruption of the native Irish word for island. The founder, St. Columba or Columcille (521-597), was of royal blood in Donegal, but he gave up everything to become a monk, a learned, efficient and very holy monk. He established three monastic schools, including that at Kells, famous for its illuminated manuscripts, and then with a party of fellow monks in 563 sailed for the island off the Scottish coast and started a monastery on it. In the eighth century it was replaced by another, whose ruins are still on the island.

Western Scotland, like Ireland, would seem to have been very receptive to Christian doctrine, for by the time of St. Columba's death the whole region was Christian. Another Irish monk, St. Aidan, founded a similar monastic settlement to St. Columba's, but on an island off the northern coast of England—Lindisfarne or Holy Island. St. Aidan had been invited to settle there by the Anglo-Saxon king of Northumbria, St. Oswald.

These Irish monks must have been adaptable people, as are all good missionaries. They did not limit their efforts to work among their fellow Celts in Scotland or to the nearby Anglo-Saxons. Two great monastic centers on the European continent owe their existence to them.

St. Columban or Columbanus was born in the south of Ireland in 543 and educated in the north. In the latter part of the sixth century he sailed for France with a party of twelve other monks and established a monastery in the Vosges. There was friction between him and the French; the local clergy quarreled with him about the date of Easter, accusing him of forcing Celtic practices on them, while the Burgundian court resented some forthright rebukes, probably well deserved, administered to the king and queen. Columban was driven out of the country, worked for a time among the still-pagan tribes in Switzerland, and then moved down to Italy. There, near the town of Bobbio in the Apennines, he founded a monastery and ruled it until his death in his seventies in the year 615. He was a learned monk and set a tradition of learning in his abbey, which in later years adopted the Benedictine rule.

One of St. Columban's associates was a monk named Callich, known to history as St. Gall. The latter had stayed in Switzerland when his friend went down to Italy, and in the Swiss forests he established a community which grew steadily until his death in 615. This was the beginning of the great monastic center of St. Gall, afterwards famed for scholarship when it had, like Bobbio, adopted the Benedictine form of life.

3. For the English-speaking Catholics of the world the most important of these missionary enterprises in the Dark Ages was the journey from St. Andrew's monastery in Rome of one Augustine with forty other monks to England. The saintly Gregory who had seen the Anglo-Saxon slave boys in the Roman slave market had been made pope and could no longer dream of going to evangelize the northern island, so he sent Augustine instead. It was a wise choice. Augustine, according to the records, seems to have been a man with personal charm and a gentle manner, a gift for diplomacy and, above all, dogged perseverance.

The party landed on the coast of Thanet, part of Kent,

in southeastern England in 597. There had been an earlier abortive start; some of the monks had lost heart at the prospect ahead of them—the stormy seas between England and the mainland, the nature of the country covered with forests and marshes and shrouded in mist and, worst of all, the sinister reputation of the people, notoriously rough and brutal. The pope managed to revive their spirits and allayed their fears with a letter to the wife of King Ethelbert of Kent, who would be their host. He was still a pagan, but his wife Berta or Bertha was a Christian, with a chapel and an attendant priest. The king, moreover, was friendly.

The mission was successful from the start. The queen and her chaplain were helpful, and before long the king was baptized and became the monks' benefactor. He had given them permission to preach even before his own conversion, and now he gave them a house and land for a church. Augustine recrossed the dreaded English Channel, went to Rome and was consecrated bishop. Five years later the pope sent him the pallium and he became the first archbishop of Canterbury (601). Two years after this the new archbishop consecrated two bishops for the new dioceses of Rochester and London. England was rapidly becoming Christian, and its native clergy was being trained on Roman lines. This led to bitterness between the English and the Celtic churchmen, one of the sorrows of St. Augustine's later years. The old British clergy were deeply attached to their own customs, and they disliked the milder religious life of these Benedictine intruders as they considered them. The archbishop invited the British bishops to a conference, but all his gentleness, suavity, and desire for good relations were of no avail. It took more than fifty years for the memory of old wrongs to die away sufficiently for a new conference, the Synod of Whitby in 664, to heal the breach between the two churches. At Whitby all the higher clergy, British and Anglo-Saxon, agreed to conform to Roman practices.

The happy outcome of the Synod of Whitby was largely due to St. Wilfrid (about 634-709), who had been trained in the Celtic practice by a monk of Lindisfarne. He had gone to France, then to Italy, and in Rome decided to adopt the Roman practices. He became archbishop of York but was driven out of his see by intrigue, restored, driven out again, and declared excommunicate by a group of disgruntled clerics. He appealed to Rome and was supported by the pope in 704. He died five years later after a life full of vicissitudes and endless labor. He was an enthusiastic builder of churches; we are told that his company when he traveled included stonemasons with their equipment. His success at Whitby makes him co-architect with St. Augustine of Canterbury of a fervent and united church among the Anglo-Saxons. Thereafter this church became in its turn a source of missionary enterprise in other lands.

Of the missionaries from Anglo-Saxon England the greatest was a monk named Wynfrith (Winfrid), better known as St. Boniface, the apostle of Germany. He was born about 680 in Devonshire, a region of seafaring men. He became a monk, was made abbot of his monastery, and then crossed the North Sea to help St. Willibrord, another English missionary monk working among the pagans of the Frisian Islands. The local king was hostile and Winfrid went to Rome, where he impressed Pope Gregory II with his learning and eloquence. The pope sent him to Germany and, later, seeing his success with the chiefs and their subjects, recalled him to Rome for episcopal consecration, having given him his new name of Boniface. The new bishop never set foot in his native land again. He was backed up in his missionary work and his administration as bishop by Charles Martel, the energetic Frankish king who was the grandfather of Charlemagne. Both king and bishop were loyal subjects of the Papacy, although it is possible the king's enthusiasm had something of political motive about it.

St. Boniface seems never to have forgotten his interlude of missionary labor with St. Willibrord among the rough islanders off the coast of Holland. In 754 he contrived to resign his high position, for he had become archbishop of Mainz, and bade farewell to his German flock. He was now an old man in his seventies, with a life of endless labor, travel, hardship, and asceticism behind him, but he set out joyfully for the Frisian Islands with some zealous companions. In the summer of the same year, 754, he and his fellow workers died as martyrs at the hands of pagan Frisians.

The massacre of this party of peaceful Benedictines is symbolical of the troublous times through which the Church was passing. The Dark Ages were growing darker. Instead of any glimpse of the dawn which still lay some three centuries ahead, there had arisen over Europe the threat of a power which apparently menaced the very existence of Christendom.

5. The Church in Peril

1. The metaphor of the Catholic Church as a ship, the bark of St. Peter, has been used so often that repetition has dulled its point; that happens with all good metaphors. A little use of our imagination may revive the metaphor. Let us picture the bark of St. Peter tossed about on a stormy sea and, so far as human judgment goes, in danger of foundering. Such was the state of the Church in the centuries when the Roman Empire was in process of disintegration and before the first Christian Renaissance of the Middle Ages. We are considering a period from about the end of the fourth century to the beginning of the twelfth.

Three terrifying threats were in existence. Sometimes one was to the fore, sometimes another: much of the time all three were active. As things overlap in secular history and are bewilderingly entangled in church history, it will help us to specify them and look at them in isolation.

First of all there was the threat of a new, active, and militant religion, the creed of Mohammed (or Mahomet) that had arisen in the Middle East. This threat hung over the minds of Christian men until the latter part of the sixteenth century, and we are its residuary legatees. Meanwhile the old menace of the barbarian invasions of Christendom, from the north and the east, still had to be reckoned with. Thirdly, and to a believing Christian the most ominous of all, was the corruption within the Church —a brutalized and often untended laity, the lesser clergy deficient in education and only too often in piety as well, the higher prelates and a number of the popes scandalous in their lives and greedy of wealth, zealous only "to scramble at the shearers' feast."

In the latter part of the sixth century—the years between 570 and 580 have been suggested—Mohammed was born in Arabia. It was about the time when a youngish Benedictine monk, whose kindly, punning humor concealed a talent for negotiation, was sent on a diplomatic mission to Constantinople. It is very unlikely that he, St. Gregory the Great, heard of the new religion being born in Arabia. He was too busy with the northern barbarians all his life and he predeceased Mohammed by nearly thirty years. The life of the Arabian "Prophet" does not concern us greatly. He seems to have been a sincere man, with strong family affections, a love of animals, and a devotion to the race from which he sprang. When he was about forty years old he claimed to have been told by God in a vision to rise from his comfortable domesticity with the wealthy but well-loved widow he had married, attack the idolatry of his people, and teach them the true faith, the Moslem faith. This was a strict unitarian monotheism that enjoined prayer and good works, especially almsgiving, and forbade usury, the use of images, spirituous drink, and the eating of pork. This last injunction, together with the rite of circumcision, Mohammed took from Judaism. Other details, to be embodied in the Koran, were of Christian origin, learned possibly from a Monophysite monk. In 622 came the

Hegira, the flight from Mecca to Medina to escape a murder plot. Ten years later the Prophet died in the arms of his last and best-loved wife, Ayesha. That might have been the end of the story of one more of the myriad cults that had arisen in the Middle East and been forgotten. It was not so. The new religion grew with a speed and vitality that seemed to rival the Christian Faith itself. It was the most formidable enemy of the Church for centuries up to the eve of the Protestant Reformation.

What happened after Mohammed's death? Simply that within about half a century the new faith, aggressive and militaristic, had taken possession of Egypt, Palestine, Persia, and Syria, besides Arabia, the country of its origin. Sixty-three years after the founder's death, that is in 695, Roman North Africa, recently Christian, had become a Moslem province. In 711, Moslem forces of the Berber race, which had been forcibly converted to the new creed, crossed the Strait of Gibraltar and overran the Spanish peninsula. Soon they had crossed the Pyrenees and were masters of southern France as well as all the Mediterranean islands except Corsica.

Pushing their way eastwards they besieged Constantinople in 717, but here they met their first setback when they were defeated by the emperor Leo III. They then began a northward movement in France, but this time they suffered a crushing defeat. At Poitiers in 732 they were beaten with great slaughter by Charles Martel ("the Hammer"). This gave heart to the people of a harassed Christendom. The Mohammedans, however, controlled the Mediterranean, the Inland Sea that had helped extend the Roman Empire and the Church; now it set a limit to such expansion. Soon the Moslems would in similar fashion be able to hamstring the Eastern (Byzantine) Empire and with it the whole of Greek-speaking Christianity.

2. Of the barbarian influx into Christian Europe which seemed at times to menace the Church's survival, we can give only an outline. Barbarian forays on the border were nothing new in the Roman Empire. As the imperial power declined, the empire's defenses were weakened. Lombards, Goths, and Visigoths overran Italy; the Vandals ravaged North Africa and the Huns pushed in from the northeast, while northern seafaring races wiped out the Romano-British civilization.

For those who were their immediate victims, perhaps the most terrifying of all were the Danes, who in the eighth and ninth centuries wrought great havoc on the Christian Anglo-Saxon civilization which had developed in England. The story of Alfred the Great's life is largely the record of his struggle with these ruthless heathen pirates, as they were originally. Alfred managed to save half his kingdom only by the sacrifice of the other half to the Danes as a Danish realm, the Danelagh, by the Treaty of Wedmore in 878. The Danes established themselves in Ireland, but they were repulsed at Paris and in what is now Belgium. As pagans they seem to have had an intense hatred for the Christian religion. Their attacks on churches, monasteries, and convents were especially brutal. After their conversion they were model Christians. Canute (Knut), the second Danish king of England, was the type and exemplar of a Christian ruler.

In nearly all cases the barbarian conquerors were soon overcome by the civilization and, above all, by the religion they seemed to be destroying. Only of the Moslems was this not true. The others were assimilated to the old Roman way of life, adopted its standards and a form of its language, and were converted to the religion of the Christian empire. Christianity had no more loyal supporters than the Lombards, the Franks, and the Anglo-Saxons after they had become Christians. This is quite intelligible. In the realm of religion they had nothing to compete with the Faith except crude tribal deities and a vague pantheon of demigods. This kind of religion withered away in the face of Christian belief and ethics, as had the old Roman polytheism.

The case is different with the faith which Mohammed had created. Here we have a system that, for those who accepted its founder's claims, was crystal clear in its simple, fervent doctrine of the One God and His prophet. Its dogmas, precepts, and prohibitions were as definite and easy to grasp as those of the Christian religion, and its ethical code was less demanding. The Moslem conquerors were never absorbed by the civilizations of the races they overcame. They might be more or less tolerant and they would adopt the secular learning and the physical amenities of the conquered lands, but they did not become one with the people. They might persecute or they might ignore Christians, but they did not, as a body, accept the Christians' beliefs.

3. The third menace to the welfare of the Church—to her continued existence, for any who had ceased to believe that Christ's words guaranteed her life for all future ages—came from within. Its story is a complex one; cause and effect are at times hard to separate. At times, also, seeming benefits have unhappy results.

Probing into remote causes we come up against the antagonism between east and west, often latent but never wholly extinct. Rome and Constantinople were the foci of two civilizations, different in language, traditions, customs. Even unity of doctrine did not always suffice to preserve harmony, and things were worse when the growing Moslem power changed the Mediterranean Sea from a highway to a barrier. Ironically enough, much mischief was caused by the misguided zeal of the eastern emperor, Leo III, to whom the Christian world was deeply indebted. This ruler had withstood the siege of his capital in 717 and thus had checked the Moslem inroads for a long time. Unfortunately he took it into his head to be theologian as well as emperor. He decided that eastern Christians paid too great reverence to religious statues and he issued an edict against their use. This was bad enough, but he went further and declared that all reverence paid to images was erroneous and sinful. This was the heresy called Iconoclasm. The parochial clergy mostly supported their emperor, but the ascetics and desert monks stood firmly in opposition. Many were tortured or executed.

A reconciliation took place after Leo's death when the empress Irene was governing as regent. Much harm had been done, however, and the fanaticism of the Iconoclasts continued to embitter relations between Rome and Constantinople. The shadow of schism seemed to hang over the eastern clergy and their rulers. There is a connection between these happenings in the eastern empire and the abuses that arose in the Church in the west. The east had lost interest in the west and was reluctant to cooperate in defense against the barbarians. When the Lombards, who had for a time been loyal to the Papacy, turned against it in the middle of the eighth century and threatened Rome itself, the eastern empire could not or would not help. The pope, Stephen III, in despair called upon the Franks. They came to his defense, drove out the Lombards, and handed the reconquered territory to the pope. He, of course, had to reward his rescuers. The Franks were nominally ruled by the descendants of Clovis, but by now these were a feeble and decadent family. Actual power, but not the title of royalty, was held by Pepin ("the Short"), son of Charles Martel, the "Hammer" of the Moslems, and father of the famous Charlemagne. The pope recognized Pepin's claim to title as well as reality of power and solemnly anointed him king of the Franks.

Two things had happened. Probably the clergy of the

time did not grasp their significance, but we see the effects, sometimes for good, often for evil. The pope had become a territorial prince as well as supreme pastor; he was the *Papa-Re* (Pope-King) and was to remain so until 1870. There had been gifts of land to the Holy See before Pepin's act, but not the formal installation of the pontiff as a territorial monarch. Secondly, the pope in this capacity was beholden to a secular ruler as benefactor, with whom he might be expected to cooperate at times. The situation was fraught with danger to his freedom of action. A king or emperor might seek to put pressure on the pope to further his own plans. Further, the papal tiara had now become, to men avid for power and wealth, one of the world's prizes. Early bishops of Rome, especially before Constantine's Edict, were saints, many of them martyrs; they had no opportunity to wield earthly power or to amass wealth.

There was trouble in 767 when a saintly pope, Paul I, died after a ten years' pontificate. A Roman military clique sought to get control of the Papacy by installing a layman named Constantine as pope. The clergy called on the Lombards, now on friendly terms with the pope again, for help; some months later the interloper was driven out.

King Pepin, who died in 768, was succeeded by his son Charles, whom we call Charlemagne or Charles the Great. On the death of Pope Stephen IV in 772 a Roman churchman of aristocratic family was elected and took the title of Adrian I. For a time all went well; it was the honeymoon period of a marriage of Church and State. The Lombards once more gave trouble; Charles and his Franks came to the rescue, and the friendship between Caesar and Christ's Vicar was strengthened. There were differences of opinion, for Charles was something of an Iconoclast and the pope formally approved the Catholic use of images, but throughout the long pontificate of more than twenty years

Adrian and Charlemagne were friends. Adrian was a good pope and a good temporal ruler, whose Roman subjects were indebted to him for an improved water supply when he brought the old aqueducts into service again.

The cloud, as yet no larger than a man's hand, on the Church's horizon is perceptible the year Adrian died. His successor, Pope St. Leo III, also a Roman, confirmed the recognition of Charlemagne as "Patrician of Rome." The king, in acknowledging the favor, added a little homily, offering paternal advice about the duties of one called on to govern. The note of patronage was ominous. The state of mind it signified was made clear a few years later when the pope barely escaped brutal rivals who would have blinded him and torn out his tongue so that he would be ineligible to function as pontiff. Charlemagne, called on for help, did not go to Rome. The pope, who had crowned Charlemagne emperor on Christmas Day, A.D. 800, went to him. Although received with honor and ceremony, Leo had to attend a kind of trial—compurgation or testimony by sponsors under oath—before the king would deal with his enemies. Clearly the king saw himself as at least the pope's equal in authority, sharing with him the responsibility for the welfare of the Church. More probably he saw himself as appointed by God as overlord of both Church and State.

Charlemagne had many attributes of greatness and he was zealous for the Church, although his zeal was not always according to wisdom. For the forcible "conversion" of the still-pagan Saxons—a policy that Clovis had followed with the Franks—he was admonished by Alcuin, the English scholar whom he had called to his court to aid him in promoting education and literature among his people. The king was a good linguist, although his mastery of writing never went very far. He was very conscious and conscientious about the illiteracy of his subjects. The low standard in this respect during the late seventh to the eleventh century was partly an effect of the Moslem advance, which about 650 cut off the supply of papyrus from the east. Paper was not yet known in Europe and parchment was very expensive. The cost of material and the slowness of copying by hand meant that few books were produced and circulated.

The period between the death of Charlemagne in 814 and the end of the tenth century was a time of violence, ruthlessness, and chaos in Europe generally and of recurrent abuses and corruption in the Church. The upper clergy and for long periods the Papacy itself were under the control of unscrupulous and even depraved worldlings. The spiritual life of the lower clergy and of the laity suffered accordingly. The priests were often apathetic, ill-educated, acquisitive, and unfaithful to the western church tradition of celibacy. It was not uncommon for bishops and other dignitaries to "marry" and then contrive to hand on their sees or other benefices to their children. The laity were too often brutish, ignorant, and at best superstitious rather than religious.

Some of the popes of this period were bad enough in all conscience, but historical truth demands that we recognize the existence of the good ones. There were several who are listed as saints in the Church's calendar. One of them, St. Nicholas I (pope from 858 to 867) stands in history as one of the truly great popes. He showed moral and physical courage in defense of the inviolability of marriage when King Lothair of Lorraine sought by threats and invasion to bully him into granting a divorce. With King Boris of Bulgaria the pope worked to organize and strengthen religious life in the king's lands. This pope showed statesmanship in dealing with the complex quarrel with Photius, the learned but acrimonious layman thrust into the bishopric of Constantinople in place of the lawful patriarch Ignatius. What started as a dispute over a see developed into the theological controversy about the *filioque* clause in the Creed. Peace was restored temporarily, but the doctrinal dispute was revived later, and in spite of two temporary reconciliations the schism between the east and Rome still persists.

We cannot say for certain whether the good popes like St. Nicholas I did more good than the unworthy ones did harm. Perhaps, had Charlemagne's sons been men of the same caliber as their father, only able and virtuous men would have been allowed to wear the pope's crown. On the other hand this would have meant perhaps a greater subordination of the Church's government to secular rulers. This was a peril warded off by the early collapse of Charlemagne's work as an empire builder. Before his death he divided his territories into three kingdoms for his three sons. Two of them died early, after a good deal of wrangling, and the survivor, Louis "the Pious," was left as both king and emperor. He in turn divided his lands among his sons, who were more quarrelsome than their uncles. All this had its effect on the Papacy. As the secular rulers became weaker, the popes became stronger; even if unworthy churchmen, they still had the added prestige over and above their temporal status of being the successors of St. Peter. Also—a cause of many evils— the Roman See became more than ever a worldly prize worth seizing.

From the death of Pope Paul I, when a junta thrust the layman Constantine on the papal throne (767), this sort of thing began. It occurred at intervals until the latter part of the eleventh century. There was, for instance, the Roman youth Octavian, Count of Tusculum, made pope as John XII in his teens by the Roman nobles in 955. He shocked the tough minds and consciences of tenth-century Europe by his immoral life. The emperor Otto "deposed" him and nominated an antipope, but John got his throne back and held it until he was murdered in 964, allegedly in a quarrel about a woman. The historian is amazed by the widespread simony, greed, violence, and moral laxity as recorded by the contemporary chroniclers, such as the monk Benedictus, who in a halting Latin that is often ungrammatical tells a story of church scandals in his time. Cardinal Newman surmised that much skepticism and even atheism often lurked under outward conformity and lip service to the Church in the early Middle Ages. Certainly there was enough corruption in high places to make this intelligible.

6. The Church in an Age of Transition

1. Belief in an infallible Church does not involve belief in the sinlessness of her ministers. The scandals of the Dark Ages and of part of the Renaissance era later on were often appalling, but we see the vitality of the Church not in the absence of scandals but in her power of recuperation, of reforming herself without losing her essential character.

In the period extending roughly from the middle of the ninth century to the middle of the eleventh the Church was beginning to emerge from a troublous time. She had been in peril from barbarian invasions, the steady progress westward of the Mohammedans, lay interference in her government, and the deplorable lives of many of her higher clergy, the bishops and the popes. The phrase Dark Ages, however, has been overworked.* Not all was bad, either in Church or State; good and evil flourished alongside each other. There were movements of reform even when things seemed to be at their worst,

* For the historian of the Catholic Church it is convenient to use the term for the period from about 500 A.D. to the beginning of the early medieval renaissance, starting about the end of the eleventh century.

and the history of the age is brightened by unexpected paradoxes, such as the favor shown to the austere monastic reform of Cluny by Pope John XII, of whom the monk-chronicler tells that *"diligebat collection (em) feminarum"* ("he was a great woman chaser"). We may note another paradox in this transitional period. Lay interference was one of the great evils of the time. Powerful families seized bishoprics and abbeys for their sons to take over without any idea of "vocation," and for generations the Papacy itself was the biggest prize. The Frankish or German potentate who was on top and soon to be Holy Roman Emperor usually saw himself as divinely set to rule both Church and Empire. It was from this unpromising background that there came the man who was to start house cleaning for the Church.

From early Christian times, men had been obsessed by the idea that the end of the world was near at hand—especially when life was more than normally nasty, brutish, and short. During the miseries of the eighth and ninth centuries the year 1000 was awaited for the consummation of all things. The German king Otto the Great (912-973) was probably too busy to brood over this. He was founding the Holy Roman Empire. He was the son of a restless Saxon monarch, Henry I, nicknamed "the Fowler," orthodox enough but what we may call an anticlerical. Otto the Great, his son and heir, was the child of his time and upbringing. He wanted a purified Church and a virtuous clergy, on the assumption that with him, by divine right, lay the responsibility for the welfare of the Church.

By mutual concessions Otto and John's predecessor, Pope Agapetus II, had got along well enough. When the worldly young duke Octavian was maneuvered onto the papal throne by his father, Otto and the new pope made a kind of offensive and defensive alliance. John crowned Otto as emperor after getting his much-needed help against his own enemies. The pope broke the treaty, doing, it seems, the right thing in the wrong way: he violated his pledge in order to free the Papacy from imperial control. Otto marched on Rome, "deposed" the pope, convoked a synod, and made it elect his own candidate as antipope Leo VIII. As soon as the emperor had left Rome, the citizens put John back and he at once excommunicated Otto and his friends. Soon after this the pope was murdered and the Romans elected Benedict V. This time the emperor carried the pope off to captivity and he died in Germany.

The next pope, John XIII, ruled in comparative peace for seven years, being submissive enough to please the emperor. Benedict VI, elected in 972, ruled for a year—long enough to crown the new emperor as Otto II—and then was strangled by his enemies. The scandals centered on the papal court were due, directly or indirectly, to the encroachment of imperial power on the authority of the Church. There were more good men than bad on the papal throne and not all the emperors were evil or unscrupulous, but a century was to pass before the man arose who would make the Papacy independent of the emperor. This man was a fearless pontiff and a saint.

2.   It is a relief to turn from the ineptitude and corruption of some of the popes to the enterprises which show that religious fervor and genuine spirituality were alive all the time. One of the great revivals of Catholic monasticism began and reached its maturity in the tenth century. In 910 a devout nobleman, Guillaume, Count of Auvergne, known as William the Pious, founded a monastery near Cluny, close to the wine-making town of Mâcon in central France. This foundation was to stand outside the feudal system, the complex social structure which became stronger as the central power of the empire grew weaker. Feudalism had a bad effect on monastic life. It

tended to make monasteries as well as bishops' sees objects of family greed. William, himself a nobleman, was able to preserve his foundation from becoming subject to feudal vassalage. More revolutionary still, he planned that it should not be subject to the bishops, who were often careerist barons, for episcopal consecration seldom made worldlings into men of God. Above its own abbot Cluny had no superior except the pope.

On the strictly religious side Cluny aimed at a return to the full observance of St. Benedict's *Holy Rule*. This included the recital in choir of the Divine Office, the *Opus Dei* (Work of God), as the *Rule* calls it, physical and mental labor for all monks, lifelong residence in the monastery under a vow of stability, and the usual vows of religious life. The asceticism and the piety of Cluny drew men of good will from all over Europe. Other religious houses begged for guidance and were affiliated to the abbey of Cluny. This gave its abbot an authority akin to that of the heads of later religious orders having centralized rule, except that under St. Benedict's scheme each community remained a family whose members stayed always under the same roof. Soon the Cluniac movement had spread to all parts of France and then south to Italy and north to Flanders. Later it established itself in Germany and England. For the Church as a whole, Cluny was a seedbed of reform. The abbey trained monks who were called from their cloister to be bishops and archbishops, in several cases popes, with high ideals of personal holiness and the will to combat simony and concubinage among the clergy.

After the Cluniac reform there were other religious leaders who sought in place of the cenobitical or community type of life on Benedictine lines a return to the eremitical or solitary life of the desert fathers. We find St. Romuald early in the eleventh century starting a hermit community, the Camaldolese, on the slopes of the

Apennines in central Italy. The monks live in separate "cells," tiny cottages, and meet only for Divine Office in a central church. St. Romuald's order is still in existence. A generation after Camaldoli, St. John Gualbert founded his order of Vallombrosians, named after Vallombrosa, in Tuscany. They followed a form of the Benedictine rule. The order is memorable for the fact that in it lay brothers, authentic monks but without the education or the desire to be priests or choir monks, now appear as a definite category of religious men under vow. In 1084 St. Bruno started a foundation of hermits, unbelievably austere, vowed originally to perpetual silence. His monastery was on a mountain near the village of Cartusia or Chartreuse, not far from Grenoble.

3.   The closing years of the eleventh century saw the beginning of one of the most important of all monastic enterprises, destined to have far-reaching effects on the life of the western world and to help build the structure of medieval Catholicism. In 1098 a certain Robert left his abbey of Molesmes in the Côte d'Or region to found a new and stricter monastery on a piece of swampy land near Dijon. His monks were called Cistercians after the name of the village of Cîteaux and became known as the White Monks* to distinguish them from the original black-habited Benedictines. Like the monks of Cluny, they were to follow the *Holy Rule* in its pristine severity, with special emphasis on manual labor, especially that needed for agriculture. Austerity marked even the church in which the monks of Cîteaux worshiped. The artistry and the imposing ritual of Cluny were replaced by an almost puritanical severity and bareness.

* The Cistercian habit is white, with a black scapular. Trappists, a strictly reformed branch of the Cistercian Order, get their name from the Abbey of La Trappe in Normandy, founded in the seventeenth century by the Abbé de Rancé, who had been a worldly courtier priest under Louis XIV.

Robert was recalled to his own abbey, and the rapid growth of the new venture began a decade later under an English abbot, St. Stephen Harding. The name of Cîteaux is associated forever with St. Bernard, who with thirty other fervent young men entered the abbey about fifteen years after its foundation. Half a dozen years later St. Norbert, a friend of St. Bernard and influenced by his example, started another order of white-robed religious in northern France, the Premonstratensian canons regular, who follow a strict version of the Augustinian rule. Unlike the Cistercians, they gave themselves largely to preaching and parochial work and did much for the revival of Christian living among clerics and laity in northern Europe, where they still have flourishing communities.

4. The wealth of ascetical and mystical life in these foundations might have failed to reform the Church in her age of transition had bishops and popes gone on being placemen of emperors or the tools of ambitious or acquisitive Roman families. That incubus had to be thrown off, and so we come to the great struggle over lay investiture, that is, the nomination or the appointment of church dignitaries, from cathedral canons to popes, by laymen.

Early in the eleventh century a saint ruled as emperor. Henry II (1002-1024) and his wife Kunegunde have both been canonized. The contemporary pope was Benedict VIII, a member of the immensely rich Theophylact family which through a number of papal reigns ran the Papacy like a family inheritance in an age of corrupt politics. Perhaps the best things about this pope are that he defeated an antipope and that he cooperated with the devout emperor in measures of reform. The emperor in all good faith continued to appoint his own candidates as bishops. The Theophylacts meanwhile kept the Papacy in the family. Pope Benedict was followed by his brother, a layman at the time, who hastily got himself ordained and consecrated and made the transition from minor orders to papal tiara in one day. A piece of church graft—there is no milder title suitable—was being planned with the patriarch of Constantinople but went too far even for that age, so the pope, John XIX, called off the deal and made friends with the emperor Conrad II, whom he crowned in St. Peter's at Easter (1027). When this pope died in 1033 he had made sure that the papal crown should stay with the Theophylacts. It was inherited by the late pope's nephew, a boy of twelve, who became Benedict IX. A pessimistic Catholic at that time might have felt that although the year 1000 had not seen the end of the world, the event could not be far off.

After a time the teen-age pope was "deposed" and an antipope put in his place. Benedict regained his throne, abdicated, and was followed by Gregory VI, who is said to have bought the position for cash. Benedict then tried again to get his throne back. Meanwhile an antipope calling himself Silvester III had appeared. Conrad's son Henry III was now emperor. He was a good soldier, forceful, energetic, earnest, and very religious in his own way, that is, seeing himself as God's anointed called upon to rule both Church and State. He was a good friend to the Cluniac reformers.

The Roman scandals shocked Henry and spurred him to action. He marched into Italy, called together the Synod of Sutri, and deposed all three claimants to the See of St. Peter. His own candidate was a zealous German bishop we know as St. Clement II. He started reforms, especially the abolition of simony,* but when the emperor had left Italy Benedict IX reappeared and Clement died soon

* Named after Simon Magus (Acts 8:9-24), who tried to buy spiritual powers from St. Peter. The word is used for the sin of trading religious privileges for money or other material goods.

after; it was said he had been poisoned. Thanks to the emperor the Papacy was saved from a further period of degradation. Damasus II, favored by Henry, had a short pontificate, and when he died in 1048 Henry III put forward as his nominee a saintly prelate, Bruno, of Alsatian birth, who was bishop of Toul. In history he lives as Pope St. Leo IX.

5. St. Leo's accession was a turning point in the history of the Papacy. The end of secular government of the Papacy as a matter of course was in sight, and a quarter of a century later would take place the contest of will and principles to settle the question forever.

Pope Leo recognized his nomination by the emperor's delegates, but would not regard himself as supreme pontiff until his canonical election by the clergy and people of Rome. He traveled down to Italy and entered Rome on foot, dressed as a pilgrim. He was elected unanimously in the accepted way—by acclamation—at Easter, 1049. At once he set to work on reforms; in 1053 he issued decrees against simony and disregard of the law of celibacy for the priesthood. His reign was saddened by the bitter friction between east and west, which became intense when his legates excommunicated the patriarch of Constantinople, Michael Caerularius, in 1054, thus paving the way for a permanent schism later on.

Much of St. Leo's life after he became pope was filled with travel and unremitting labor. He went about Europe, holding conferences, reforming abuses and encouraging monastic life, especially the Cluniac monasteries. His last years were spent in defending his subjects against Norman aggression, and he died in 1054 after leading an army, unsuccessfully, against the invaders. One of his devoted assistants in the work of reform had been an austere monk, Pietro Damiani (St. Peter Damian) whom Leo made a cardinal. St. Peter wrote a book denouncing abuses among the clergy—simony, avarice, unchastity—as he had come across them in the work of reform. This *Liber Gomorrhianus* (Book of Gomorrah) is, perhaps, the most terrible indictment of evil men ever written by a saint.

The emperor Henry III died a few years after the death of his fellow reformer Pope St. Leo IX. The imperial crown passed to Henry's infant son who, as Henry IV, was growing to an early maturity during the four brief pontificates after St. Leo's reign. The most important event for the Papacy in these years was the enactment of the law that future popes should be elected by the cardinals.* The last of these four popes, Alexander II (1061-1073), had trouble with a rival put forward by a clique of wealthy Roman laymen who wished to keep their hold on the Papacy. A council supported the legitimate pope, but it was a council called together by imperial edict.

6.   When St. Leo in his humble pilgrim's dress had gone down to Italy in 1049 as the choice of the emperor's delegates, he had with him as secretary a young Italian monk in deacon's orders named Ildebrando. He was a Benedictine, but a friend and admirer of the Cluniac monks. Historians know him as Hildebrand and the Catholic Church honors him as St. Gregory VII.

The young emperor Henry IV had already taken over the personal control of his dominions when Hildebrand, who had been made a cardinal by St. Leo III, was elected pope in 1073. Henry resented the election of the reforming cardinal, already known as the foe of simony and

* The cardinals, who may be priests, bishops, archbishops, or, occasionally in former times, laymen, are the highest ecclesiastical dignitaries below the pope. The "College" of Cardinals as a distinct body of church officials is the result of a gradual process of development. As early as the fifth century we find the word *cardinal* (from the Latin for a hinge) used for the priests in charge of the chief parish churches in Rome. Being directly under the pope and in close proximity to him, they be‧ came a senate or advisory council to aid him in government.

clerical concubinage and now ready to fight for the end of lay investiture. At the moment Henry was dealing with a rebellion of his turbulent Saxon subjects, and he kept the peace with the new pope. It did not last very long. Henry broke his promises, thrust his nominees in the sees of bishops and archbishops, and tried to get together a synod of episcopal yes-men to pronounce the pope "deposed." This time the tactic failed. The imperial decree was received with violent anger in Rome, and only the pope's intervention saved the life of the priest who came as the emperor's messenger.

St. Gregory VII, called by his election to cultivate a tough mind and a will of steel in his fight for freedom and supremacy of the See of St. Peter, was one of those small, kindly, peace-loving men who seem to be made for the seclusion and tranquil round of monastic duties. He excommunicated the emperor, declared him deposed, and absolved all imperial subjects from their allegiance. Meanwhile a council of the suzerain princes would choose a successor. Henry had been getting the better of the rebellious Saxons, but now the latter joined themselves to the princes who were prepared to obey the pope. They decided that if the emperor was still under the ban within a year he should be replaced.

Henry was in a quandary. He was angry and his pride was wounded, but he chose the lesser of two evils, swallowed his pride, and accepted the necessary humiliation —the famous penance at Canossa. The pope was on his way north to join the council of princes and he stopped at Canossa, a mountain stronghold in Emilia belonging to his friend Matilda, Countess of Tuscany, the "Great Countess," an amazing woman who by marriage was related to one of the previous popes and helped four others in fighting abuses, ruled her own territories, and kept up correspondence with scholars and theologians, including St. Anselm. To her castle came the emperor Henry and his wife, seeking papal clemency, absolution, and the raising of the ban of excommunication. The emperor, barefoot and in the coarse shirt of a penitent, waited for three days in the January mountain snows at the door of the castle. Finally he was admitted to the pope's presence, at the petition, it is said, of the countess.

Gregory gave the emperor absolution and lifted the ban, but was skeptical of the ruler's crocodile tears and promises of good behavior. The skepticism was soon seen to be justified. Henry violated the ban on appointing bishops and won a majority of German prelates to his side. The princes supporting the pope appointed a successor to the imperial throne, Rudolph of Suabia, but he died on the battlefield and Henry gained the upper hand, assembled an army, and marched on Rome, to "depose" Gregory and set up his own nominee. Rome was surrendered by treachery, but the pope took refuge in the Castel Sant' Angelo, formerly Hadrian's tomb, and called for his new allies, the Normans, to help him. They arrived, drove off the imperial forces, but sacked Rome and took the pope away with them, ostensibly as guest and ally, really in what we call protective custody. Henry's antipope was enthroned in Rome, and a year later Pope St. Gregory VII died in exile at Salerno. Tradition tells us that his last words were, "I have loved justice and hated iniquity, therefore I die in exile."

An interregnum of about two years followed Gregory's death and then Pope Victor III reigned, for a few months only. The great battle over lay investiture was not over, but the Papacy had won a moral victory. Violence and usurpation would crop up again and again, but the supremacy of the pope was becoming part of the accepted and unquestioned Catholic tradition.

Henry's antipope was kept on his throne by armed forces which also served to keep the legitimate pope out of his own city. This puppet, with the title of Clement III, was still in Rome in 1088 when a great medieval church‑man was elected as the rightful pontiff. This pope was Odo (or Eude) of Cluny, who took the title of Urban II (1088-1099). He was beatified * by Pope Leo XIII in 1881. Urban had been a friend of St. Gregory VII and a fellow worker with him in church reform. His pontificate was full of troubles, and it was only a couple of years before his death that he was able to take possession of his see, when the Crusaders on their way south drove out the antipope Clement. It is in connection with the Crusades that Blessed Urban II is best known to readers of history.

7. The Crusades have a whole literature to themselves. The early nineteenth-century romantics saw them as wholly idealized. Later writers, influenced by Marxism, see them as colonialism and banditry, disguised as reli‑gious zeal. Both extremes are false. There were shameful happenings enough, such as a Jewish pogrom, unpro‑voked, shocking the consciences of good men. St. Bernard protested against the vileness. There were the atrocities in Constantinople which marked the Fourth Crusade, when the Crusaders allowed themselves to be diverted from their goal in Palestine and engaged in looting and mas‑sacre around the cathedral of the Holy Wisdom. Pope In‑nocent III, appalled by the butchery of the Byzantine citizens, schismatics but Christians with a common interest in repelling the Mohammedans, excommunicated the murderers. The horrrors of the Children's Crusade in 1212, perpetrated by the slave traders who took advantage of the naïve dreams of the victims, still, seven and a half centuries later, are as harrowing to read about as accounts of Belsen or Vorkuta.

* Beatification is the process by which the Church proclaims the sanctity of one of her members after his death. It precedes *canonization,* which formally gives the title "saint." Not all beatifications, however, are fol‑lowed by canonization.

When all has been said, it remains true that the Crusades had their origin in the idealism of the people in medieval Christendom. Reverence for places hallowed by the Savior's life, passion, and resurrection and pilgrimages to such spots had been a feature of Christian devotion from the earliest times. Modern men, even earnest believers, except perhaps for a small number of authentic mystics, find it difficult to enter into the medieval mind as it concerned itself with the Person of Jesus Christ. At its best the attitude of the medieval Christian was one of intense and passionate devotion, a romantic passion if we rescue the adjective from its present-day debasement. We see it embodied, for example, in the hymn attributed to St. Bernard and so popular in the Middle Ages, *Jesu dulcis memoria* ("Jesus, the very thought of Thee"). When the Moslems threatened Christian life in the west and the holy places were in Saracen territory, it was natural that devout men and, of course, a camp following of adventurers and mere go-getters should respond to the call for action.

Pope Urban II, saint and statesman, did more than canalize a widespread religious emotion. Of such able pontiffs as St. Leo IX, St. Gregory VII, and Blessed Urban II, we may truly say that they alone, in a chaotic Europe whose rulers were often uneducated or only semiliterate, had what we should call a foreign policy. The character and achievements of St. Gregory VII, who was followed after a short interval by Urban II, had erased the memory of papal scandals and given the Papacy prestige as moral exemplar and as bulwark against injustice and lay tyranny. Urban II was listened to and supported enthusiastically when he preached the first Crusade in 1095.*

* *Crusade*, from the Latin *crux*, a cross, refers to the cross presented to those who vowed themselves to the work. A cross was then stitched or embroidered on their outer garments. The number of Crusades is given as either eight or nine, according to the view taken of the last campaign

Kept out of Rome by the antipope supported by imperial arms, Urban had been going from place to place, calling clergy and laity together for works of reform. He was helped by Matilda of Tuscany, the "Great Countess" who had been St. Gregory VII's friend. One of these meetings of the faithful took place at Clermont, the modern Clermont-Ferrand, in the early winter of 1095. The assembly of bishops, abbots, and other clergy was followed by a public meeting held in the open fields because no building in the little city could accommodate all the people who thronged to it.

The event was impressive. Chroniclers who were present have left us many details; they have even given us a verbatim report of Pope Urban's speech. A tall, vigorous man in his early fifties, blond and bearded, he had the advantage of eloquence and a resonant voice. Like many great churchmen, he had personal charm and a gracious manner that predisposed men in his favor.

The pope did not use Latin, the international medium of clerics, but the Romance language, early French, which was understood by most of his hearers. He made an impassioned appeal for the rescue of the holy places, above all Christ's sepulcher, from desecration by the fanatical Seljuk Turks who had dispossessed the more tolerant Arabs. Spiritual privileges, above all a plenary indulgence,* were offered to all who "took the cross," even though they might never reach their goal. It was, however, a venture for hardy men and soldiers; the aged and infirm and women, unless with their husbands, were not to go on Crusade. When the pope ended his appeal, there was a tremendous ebullition of feeling. Knights and men-at-

(1271-1272), which ended in a truce with the Moslems. The Children's Crusade of 1212 was an abortive venture ending in tragedy.
* A remission of all the temporal punishment due for sins that had been forgiven. An indulgence that is not *plenary* remits some specified portion of such temporal punishment.

arms drew their swords and brandished them over their heads, and a great shout arose, *"Dieu lo veult"* ("God wills it"), which became from that time the motto of all Crusaders.

Several points should be noted about the beginnings of this movement, which was to be a feature of medieval Catholic life for many generations. First of all, whatever the later abuses, it started as a work of piety, an expression of the intense and widespread devotion to the Person of Christ which runs through all the spiritual life of the Middle Ages. Secondly, it was exclusively the work of the reformed Papacy; there were no kings in the first Crusade. The two who might have been expected to help were excommunicated—the emperor for illicit lay investiture, and Philip I of France for his repudiation of his lawful wife so that he could make a second marriage banned by the Church. Lastly, we may see in the response to Urban more than a tribute to his own force and charm. It was a sign also of the popular regard and affection for the Papacy. Able and holy pontiffs had taken the Keys of St. Peter from unworthy hands and made it clear that the pope was truly a father to Christians and the servant of the servants of God. The upsurge of crusading zeal, often mixed with less devout emotions, was revived by various popes after Urban II. The last—and inconclusive—Crusade came to an end in the closing years of the thirteenth century.

7. The Church in the Middle Ages:

St. Bernard

1. The term *medieval* is somewhat vague. To establish a perspective on a wide sweep of medieval history it may be of help to select some of its outstanding figures. These are saints and of great importance in shaping the events of their time. We shall first consider St. Bernard of Clairvaux (1090-1153), whose life falls approximately in the first half of the twelfth century, as symbol and in part the agent of the revival of spiritual life that followed the rise of a zealous and purified Papacy.

2. Ten years before the end of the eleventh century, during the pontificate of Urban II, a boy was born in a distinguished family near Dijon, baptized Bernard, and thereafter orphaned when his father died as a Crusader. In the perspective of history we can see the promise of things to come. Some ten years earlier two men, one a future saint, the other a future intellectual but no saint, had been born. The saint was St. Norbert, a German, founder of the Premonstratensians and reformer of religious life. The intellectual was Peter Abelard, a Frenchman. While Bernard was still a baby, St. Anselm, theologian and mystic, was called from his abbey in France to become archbishop of Canterbury (1093).

When Bernard was old enough to be learning his Latin grammar, Robert of Molesmes had already started his community at Cîteaux. After Robert had handed over its direction to St. Stephen Harding, Bernard had started his higher studies at Châlons. A cathedral school at that time was often the nucleus of a university, so we may take it that Bernard's family were relying on the young man's being equipped for high office in the Church; a knight-Crusader's son would be entitled to such. Bernard had other ideas. In his early twenties he set out to join the young and severely ascetic community under its English abbot at Cîteaux. Not only that; he took along with him thirty other fervent young men—four brothers and a group of his friends. When he reached his prime, he would stand above all the men of his epoch. Sternly ascetic, mystical, a genius in administration and diplomacy, and withal of deep interior humility, he dominates the ecclesiastical and spiritual life of the twelfth century.

Within a few years of his entering Cîteaux the young monk, with the support of his abbot, moved to the northeast of France and started the abbey of Clairvaux (1115), most renowned of all Cistercian centers. Under its young abbot-founder it was the spiritual powerhouse of the Church during the reigns of eight popes.

3.   Four years after St. Bernard had settled at Clairvaux a new religious order was started. It was an innovation in religious life. The members not only vowed themselves to poverty, chastity, and obedience, but they were committed to a soldier's life of fighting, marching, wounds, and death on active service if need be. The failure of the first Crusade to overthrow the Moslems in Palestine led to the foundation of these fighting monks to help the Christian pilgrims. Such was the origin of the Knights-

Templars. Within a decade they had won approval and the time had come for formal recognition. At the Synod of Troyes (1128), Bernard, who had been very busy on two of his books, *De Diligendo Deo* (On Loving God) and *De Gratia* (On Divine Grace), was invited by the cardinal-protector of the new soldier-monks to help in their organization. The saint's influence won papal recognition for them, and it is said that he drew up their rule of life for them.

The death of Pope Honorius II in 1130 was followed by a disputed election, with an antipope claiming the tiara. Louis VI ("the Fat") assembled the Synod of Etampes to decide between the claims of Innocent II, elected by the majority of the cardinals, and his rival, who took the title of Anacletus II. St. Bernard won the decision for Innocent, who was soon "accepted by the world," says the saint. France, England, Germany, and Spain all gave their allegiance to Innocent, but for a time Anacletus held out in Rome. King Louis' successor, Lothair III, met the pope and St. Bernard and made friends with both. The pope, more timorous or less clear-sighted than the saint, was for negotiation with the antipope, but Bernard opposed this. Anacletus was excommunicated, although he had been supported by the Norman Robert of Sicily. Innocent duly crowned Lothair in St. Peter's. The antipope died in 1138.

Running through the history of this period is the record of warfare, intrigue, and assassination connected with the quarrel between Guelfs and Ghibellines. The Guelfs were the papal party, the Ghibellines the supporters of the emperor, although the thing started as a dynastic contest between rival German families, with the dukes of Saxony and Bavaria opposed to the Hohenstaufens. A temporary peace had been made in 1135, again an achievement of St. Bernard, who at Bamberg persuaded Frederick Hohenstaufen to submit to the emperor.

When the antipope Anacletus died in 1138 another usurper, Cardinal Conti, who called himself Victor IV, was put in his place. St. Bernard meanwhile had been preaching in northern Italy and narrowly avoided being made a successor to St. Ambrose as archbishop of Milan; his unwillingness was so strong that Innocent II gave way. The saint came to the help of the Papacy in its contest with the new antipope. St. Bernard by his personal influence won Victor's resignation.

Some historians, including Lord Acton, consider that in the middle years of the twelfth century the abbey of Clairvaux overshadowed Rome itself. The popularity of St. Bernard's severe form of Benedictinism accounts for the great increase in the number of its monasteries—ninety-three founded or affiliated to the mother house in the period 1130-1145.

Probably it was during Innocent's pontificate, about 1140, that Gratian produced his *Decretum*. This book, by a writer of whom we know nothing except that he was probably one of the hermit-monks of Camaldoli, is an organized summary of church law. It was used as the basis of the *Codex* of canon law which, with revisions, has been the permanent code of church government.

Three years after he had, by charm or strength of will, rid the Church of an antipope, St. Bernard was the agent of Abelard's errors being condemned. The stormy career of Peter Abelard (1079-1142) and his love affair with the beautiful and learned Héloise have captured the imagination of later ages. St. Bernard, however, was concerned with the brilliant ex-professor of philosophy as a teacher whose rationalistic ideas were tinged with heresy and dangerous to orthodox belief in the Holy Trinity. The antagonism was one of temperament as well as of thought. St. Bernard, ascetic and mystic, was essentially the believer; Abelard, although he lived and died a Catholic, had the skeptical, analytic mind always suspect to the mystic.

Certain of Abelard's teachings were condemned at a council held at Sens. The philosopher appealed to Rome, but there, too, St. Bernard's influence prevailed and the condemnation was upheld. Abelard, an unhappy man broken in health and spirit, set out to appeal in person, but his sufferings were too much for him and he died in a French priory in the spring of 1142.

By 1145 the influence of the abbey of Clairvaux was at its highest point. The abbot had sought only obscurity, penance, and prayer when as a young man he joined St. Stephen Harding's monks at Cîteaux. The papal election of 1145 gave the tiara to a friend and fellow monk of St. Bernard, a Pisan who was abbot of a monastery in Rome. He took the title of Eugenius III. He, like so many of his contemporaries, looked to St. Bernard for advice and guidance. We get a hint of the esteem in which St. Bernard's opinions were held from a wry complaint in one of his letters. People pester him, he says, as though he and not his friend were pope. At this time the pope and the bishops were disturbed by the heretical propaganda of Henry of Lausanne in the south of France. We know little of this man. He seems to have been a renegade monk with ideas similar to those of the Albigensian heresy, leading to moral anarchy and the repudiation of all church authority. It is likely that the Albigenses, named after the town of Albi, took some of their doctrines from Henry of Lausanne. St. Bernard was sent to the region where the trouble was brewing and did much to keep the people faithful to orthodox teaching. We may note that he was averse from using force for what could be done by persuasion.

Pope Eugenius took refuge with St. Bernard at Clairvaux when the revolt of Arnold of Brescia, a priest of austere life but fanatical opposition to the Papacy, had a temporary success in Rome. Arnold justifiably raised his voice against abuses in clerical life, but his spirit of insubordination was anathema to St. Bernard. Eventually he was overcome, condemned, and executed.

Bad news from the east disturbed the harassed pontiff at this time. The Moslems were regaining the ascendancy and had captured the key town of Edessa, in the northwest of Mesopotamia, which had been wrested from them by the first Crusaders in Urban II's time. Pope Eugenius called on St. Bernard for help, and the saint preached the second Crusade at Vézelay in central France early in 1146. King Louis VII at once took the cross, and St. Bernard then traveled about France, Flanders, and Germany, arousing great enthusiasm and winning many recruits. Their zeal at one time took the un-Christian form of attacking the Jews of Mainz; the pillage and murder were stopped by St. Bernard's intervention. On Christmas Day he won his most unexpected recruit, Conrad III, the Hohenstaufen "king of the Romans"; St. Bernard, perhaps with a touch of irony, called this a miracle. This second Crusade cost much loss of life and treasure, but it failed to retake Edessa, and the outcome was a deep sorrow to St. Bernard and his friend Pope Eugenius.

A meeting held at Chartres and presided over by Abbot Suger made plans to retrieve the situation, the assembled Crusaders voting for St. Bernard to lead them. He was now nearly sixty, worn out by incessant labor and his own stern asceticism. Happily for the Church and for posterity, the Cistercian abbots vetoed the plan. The saint went back to his cloister and wrote for the pope the treatise *De Consideratione ad Clericos,* a guide for churchmen, and continued to send to his friends and correspondents the many letters in the excellent Latinity that has won for the writer the title of the Mellifluous Doctor. To this period belongs also a biography of the Irish reformer-bishop St. Malachy, whom St. Bernard had aided with advice on a Cistercian foundation in Ireland. In 1148 St. Malachy died at Clairvaux while on a visit to his friend.

St. Bernard himself died in 1153, that is, halfway through the twelfth century, but he dominates the whole century of what we call the medieval Renaissance.

During the saint's last years the struggle between Papacy and Empire began again. In the year before St. Bernard's death the emperor Frederick I, nicknamed Barbarossa or Redbeard, acceded to the imperial throne. His ideas were absolutist and he saw himself as divinely appointed to govern both Church and State. As Constantine's successor he was, he claimed, emperor of the Romans and above the pope. While the English pope Adrian IV (Nicholas Breakspear) was alive the contest did not go to extremes. Adrian was a determined and able pontiff who upheld his position without open hostilities. On his death trouble began. After marching into Rome the emperor, with the help of a few disgruntled cardinals, set up an antipope. The lawfully elected candidate, a learned Sienese canon lawyer, Bandinelli, who had been a trusted servant of the late pope, Adrian, took the name of Alexander III. He had to flee to France and in spite of many difficulties ruled the Church with real statesmanship. Germany, under its absolutist emperor, was in schism, but the pope kept France and England loyal to himself. Henry II of England, in his quarrel with the archbishop of Canterbury, St. Thomas à Becket, had been responsible, perhaps not intentionally, for the archbishop's murder. Popular feeling ran so high that the king found it advisable to make his peace with his own subjects and with the pope and did penance at the tomb of the dead archbishop.

Another victory for the Papacy had been won through the pope's support of the pro-papal Lombard League, which in 1176 defeated the emperor in battle and he was more than ready to make his peace with both pope and League.

Pope Alexander died in 1181. For twenty-five years he

had ruled the Church with strength of will, but also with wisdom and forbearance. He was followed by a succession of ineffective pontiffs, five of them in seventeen years, all of them elderly men, tired, unenterprising, unassertive when on the papal throne. One of them was unwise enough to favor a marriage of the youthful Henry, Barbarossa's heir, to Constance, the heiress of Sicily. A couple of years after this the emperor Frederick joined the third Crusade and died in the course of it, probably drowned in Asia Minor on his way to Palestine (1190). In 1191 a papal conclave met and elected as pope an ecclesiastic of the Orsini family, Giacinto Bobone. This pope, Celestine III, was eighty-five at the time; the king of Germany, Henry VI, was twenty-six, ambitious, energetic, unscrupulous. The outlook for the Church was grim. Henry, crowned amid much pomp by the reluctant and fearful old pontiff, lived up to the worst fears of the churchmen. He ravaged Italy, including the papal territories, wherever he met opposition, appointed and deposed bishops, punished rebels with ruthlessness, and was suspected of complicity in the murder of a bishop. The clergy saw the hand of God in the fever which killed the emperor while he was hunting in Sicily in the fall of 1197.

The worried old pope Celestine III died in 1198, and this time the conclave's vote had a happier outcome. The cardinal who was chosen was comparatively young—under forty—and besides being learned in theology and canon law he was deeply religious. His accession to the papal throne ended a seventeen-year period of unrest, uncertainty, and violence which had threatened to undo all the work of St. Gregory VII, Urban II, and Eugenius III.

8. The Church in the Middle Ages:

Two Friar Saints

1. Cardinal Lotario di Segni was elected pope early in the year 1198, on the day when old Pope Celestine III died, and took the title of Innocent III. He was not yet in priest's orders, although learned in theology and church law and the author of three books on religious subjects. Immediately after his election he was ordained a priest and consecrated a bishop. The Church and Catholic Europe were entering an era of brilliant achievement. If the twelfth century was the seed time, the thirteenth saw the harvest.

When Innocent was crowned, the outlook was bright. The troublemaker, Frederick I (Barbarossa), was dead; his son and heir had, after a brief reign, been cut off by fever and now the emperor-to-be, still an infant, was the pope's ward.

The new pope could see himself as happy in what, as head of the Church, he inherited. A number of able pontiffs, several of them saints, had raised the prestige of their office and made men forget past scandals. Gratian and his pupils had given Rome her great body of law. Educated laymen and clerics, thanks to monastic centers like Cluny and Bec and the rise of universities like that of Paris, were taking the place of illiterate nobles and ignorant priests. This was also an age of building; the mere list of *some* of the cathedrals built or begun in the era of Gothic is impressive: Angoulême, Angers, Senlis, Notre Dame (Paris), Sens, Soissons, Wells, Bourges, Chartres.

Philosophical thought was stimulated by interest in the writings of Aristotle. This, at first, was looked at askance by the bishops, for Aristotle came to the schools through what they saw as tainted channels, translations from Mohammedan versions. Theology had, meanwhile, been enriched by the books of a scholar and saint who became a successor to the missionary monk Augustine as archbishop of Canterbury, Anselm.

Most important of all in this period, the spiritual life for which the Church exists seems to have taken on a new dynamic quality. It is apparent in the spread of popular devotions based on the life of Christ, particularly that of the Five Wounds. Nor was Rome unmindful of the heathen on the frontiers of what was then the civilized world. Missionaries had been at work when the Teutonic and Slavic peoples were still pagan, and a Catholic bishopric had been established as far north as Greenland.

2. In the early years of Innocent's pontificate two events of great moment for the future of the Church took place, but doubtless were unnoticed in the world at large. In the first decade of the 1300s a boy was born in an aristocratic German family. He was named Albert and in our histories is known as Albertus Magnus ("the Great"), teacher of a yet greater pupil, Thomas of Aquino. These two men may be said to have shaped Catholic philosophy for all the centuries that have gone by since their time. We may note, as a detail of the picture of the age, that while the German infant was growing into boyhood, an ex-soldier from the Crusades, Berthold, settled with a

few friends as hermit-monks on Mount Carmel in Palestine, thus beginning the Carmelite order, a future nursery of saints and scholars.

The second significant event took place about the time of Albert the Great's birth. A young Italian, Giovanni de Bernardone, was on a visit to Rome. He had been a gay young fellow in his native Umbrian town, Assisi, where he was nicknamed "the Frenchman" (*Francesco*) because he aped the French fashions of the day. Some desultory soldiering, a brief term as a prisoner of war in one of the minor wars between Italian hill towns, and then an illness had been followed by a "conversion" to piety and the desire for a dedicated life. This was not in accordance with the ideas of businessman Pietro, the young man's father. In Rome the busy pontiff, Innocent III, arbiter of dynastic claims and fighter for papal rights, found time to listen to the visitor, then in his twenties, as he sought approval of a new community of humble brethren (friars-minor). They were to act literally on Christ's counsel to sell all and give to the poor; for themselves they would choose the dress of Umbrian peasants and feed on the broken meats begged from other men's tables. The pope gave his permission by word of mouth and five years later (1215) formally allowed the institution of the order of Friars-Minor.

Several years after his visit to Rome the *Poverello* ("the little poor man"), as he called himself, was preaching among the people in his native Umbria one day to a congregation in which was a beautiful young girl—eighteen at the time—from a noble family. She went up to the preacher after the discourse and begged to be initiated into the life of poverty and devotion; so, dressed in a white bridal costume, she presented herself in the little chapel used by the friars, had her hair shorn of its abundant locks, and then put on a rough, homespun religious habit. This young patrician was Clara, the St. Clare who thus started the austere, contemplative order named after her.

Roughly contemporary with the birth of the Franciscan order was the beginning of the Order of Preachers or Dominicans. As in the case of other orders, its start was a modest one, almost casual. About 1205 the bishop of an obscure Spanish diocese was in Rome on his way back to Spain after a diplomatic mission. With him was one of his canons, Dominic Guzman. Bishop and canon were zealous churchmen, eager for missionary work among the still-pagan Magyars and Slavs on the frontiers of Europe. Innocent III has been branded as harsh and autocratic by some historians; certainly he could lash fools and knaves with invective not heard in the Vatican today, but he was always alert to the presence of human goodness and genuine zeal. Accordingly he gave a friendly hearing to the two Spanish clerics, but he had work for them nearer home than the missionary field they had in mind. In whole areas of southern France and northern Italy orthodox faith and practice were being eroded by forms of the old Manichaean dualism which had captured the mind of the young Augustine before his conversion. At the risk of oversimplifying a complex subject we may say that this heresy is the belief in two Creators, warring with each other until a consummation, when the good one, who has created the spiritual universe, will finally overcome the evil one, who has made all material being. In this theology, spirit alone was good, all material things evil. The whole system, which might appear to be only a metaphysical nightmare, had disastrous consequences in social life. Marriage and above all the procreation of children were contemned. Celibacy became an imperative, not merely a counsel. As the life of the body was utterly evil, death, even by suicide, was preferable. All this was too much for the ordinary workaday believer. He was allowed to go his own crass way, saved on his deathbed by the *consolamentum,* a substitute for baptism.

The spiritual life of absolute continence, renunciation, and poverty was embraced by the "perfect," who were called upon to live up to the doctrine in its entirety. One can see what a corrosive force the thing could become and why various popes, including Innocent III, were worried by the spread of the heresy. As the Manichaean dualism was the outstanding feature of twelfth- and thirteenth-century heresy, it was usual for most novelties of doctrine and ethics to be branded as Manichaean. Some of the new movements, however, were at first little more than protests against laxity and corruption. This seems to be true of the Waldenses, named for their founder, Peter Waldo of Lyons, who started as a clerical reformer. His "poor men of Lyons" drifted away from Catholic doctrine and ended up as puritans, with some ideas that anticipated Protestantism.

St. Bernard by his preaching had done something to combat the spread of the Manichaean heresy, but since his time the number of its adherents had grown again. It was becoming solidly established, with local rulers sympathetic or at least neutral. Although the sectaries, known variously as Cathari (the "pure ones"), Patarins and, from the name of the city of Albi in southern France, Albigensians, were in theory pacifists, they were willing for the still-imperfect "believers" to back their evangel with force. For a long time the Papacy and its envoys, first St. Bernard and his Cistercians, then the Spanish bishop and his canon, Dominic, sought to make headway by friendly persuasion, public disputations, and other nonviolent means. Example as well as preaching was needed, said St. Dominic. If the "perfect" among the heretics could practice apostolic poverty and austerity, the missionaries must do likewise, hence their journeys on sandaled feet instead of on horseback, coarsely woven habits in place of a prelate's robes, the food and lodging of mendicants rather than a place at noblemen's tables. After a time St. Dominic's followers were formally instituted as a religious order, with the white habit under a long black cloak which gave them their medieval name of the Black Friars.

The peaceful propaganda was ended by a crime that led to the worst blood bath in medieval history. Early in 1208 a papal legate accompanied by a bishop went to Provence to persuade the local ruler against helping the sectaries. The legate was murdered by an old soldier. The murderer may have been insane, and anyhow the dying legate pardoned him, but the incident led the pope to proclaim a crusade against the heretics, with all the privileges of "taking the cross." The expeditionary force, manned and commanded chiefly by northern French barons and their feudal retainers, set out in the summer of 1209. They went down the Rhone valley in a campaign of looting, arson, and massacre. Nominally the army was under the aegis of the Papacy, with two bishops in command. Actually it soon got out of hand, for the troops were intoxicated by the wealth and amenities of Provence and the luxury of southern cities and, of course, they persuaded themselves that their orgy of frightfulness was an act of piety. Evidence exists that Innocent III, a humane and civilized ecclesiastic, was disturbed and unhappy about reports of the tempest he had let loose.

The most important event of the time in connection with the fight against heresy was the assembling of the twelfth ecumenical (universal) Council, the fourth Lateran Council (1215), which marks the zenith of papal prestige in the Middle Ages. The Council was attended by several hundred bishops, many other dignitaries such as abbots and priors, and by delegates from lay rulers. New plans were made for dealing with the various forms of Manichaeism, especially the teachings of the Waldenses and the Cathari. Here we come to the origins of the Inquisition, which has called forth much controversial writing, some of it greatly colored by emotion. There is a good deal of misunderstanding about its early phase.

The members of the Council were convinced that the systematic preaching of false doctrine called for new methods of campaign, so they took the matter out of the hands of the local bishops and planned for action directed from Rome and carried out by selected members of the new mendicant orders of friars. As time went on, the Franciscans dropped out of the work and the "inquisitions" or interrogations were left to the Dominicans; the chief reason was that the Preachers had come to be regarded as an order of theological specialists. In contrast with later penalties, the greatest punishments arranged by the Council were confiscation of goods and banishment. The death sentence was not introduced until many years later, and for a long time various popes condemned torture to obtain confessions or retractions. No Catholic has to feel he is on unsafe ground in repudiating this form of man's inhumanity to man or the later abomination of a rule, made worse by hypocrisy, that required the presence of clerical Inquisitors in the torture chamber, who might then, being forbidden by their status to shed blood, hand over the victim to the secular arm for the final penalty by fire.

Two points, matters of authentic history, should be made. The Inquisition did not arise, fully organized, from the decrees of the fourth Lateran Council. In the second place, although St. Dominic was at the Council, he had no part in framing the rules for the Inquisition, *nor did he ever serve as an Inquisitor*. Like St. Bernard before him, he combined zeal for orthodoxy with attachment to pacific ways of working for it. The use of coercion to seek out or punish heresy can be traced to the fourth century A.D. and it should be more generally known that the first great heresy trial ending in a sentence of death by fire caused shocked dismay and disapproval in two great saints, Ambrose of Milan and Martin of Tours. In an earlier age St. Augustine, calling for the suppression of Manichaean propaganda, specified a "tempered severity" only, while St. Chrysostom, wishing to safeguard the faith of simple people, desired to restrict the freedom of heretics to spread their errors, but branded the killing of these men as "an inexpiable crime."

The year (1215) before Innocent III's death is memorable for the establishment of St. Francis' Friars-Minor and for the assertion of papal power in England, where King John's obduracy had been broken by excommunication, interdict, and the threat of deposition. The redoubtable Stephen Langton (Cardinal) was the pope's choice for archbishop as against the king's nominee. The cardinal-archbishop stood with the barons when they forced their shifty, unscrupulous monarch to sign the *Magna Carta.*

3. Two birthdays in the first quarter of the thirteenth century were to add to the glory of the medieval Church. In 1221 a male child, John, was born near Viterbo. He is St. Bonaventure, the Seraphic Doctor, theologian, mystic, and one of the great Scholastics. The name by which we know him stems from the tradition that St. Francis, gazing on the child destined to become one of the greatest of his spiritual sons, exclaimed, *"Buona ventura!"* ("Good fortune!"). The other birthday, in the time of Pope Honorius III, is that of Thomas of Aquino (St. Thomas Aquinas). The Angelic Doctor was born, probably in 1225, in his father's family seat, part fortress, part mansion, of Roccasecca, in a cleft in the mountains between Rome and Naples.

In 1227, after the death of Pope Honorius III, the

conclave of cardinals voted for another churchman of the caliber of Innocent III. This was Ugolino Conti di Segni, learned and virtuous and already an expert administrator. He is thought to have been a nephew of Innocent III. Frederick II was now emperor, a subtle, complex personality, erudite, cultured, and only doubtfully a Christian believer. He had kept the peace with Pope Honorius, although rebuked for failure to live up to the Crusader's vow he had made. The new pope, Gregory IX, threatened excommunication and Frederick set out for the east, but like others who have gone on their travels, he came back in a worse frame of mind. Contact with the Moslems, it is said, had weakened his Catholic faith, and he is reported to have made a mock of Christian marriage by setting up a harem of wives and concubines in oriental fashion. His friendship with Moslem and Jewish men of learning may have been quite innocent, but was interpreted as a sign of anti-Christian sympathies.

Pope Gregory IX and this enigmatic prince were reconciled at various times, but reconciliation was always followed by the emperor's giving some new cause for offense. At the time the pope died, Frederick, once more excommunicated, was about to launch an attack on Rome. Pope Celestine IV survived his election less than three weeks and then there was a lapse of two years without a pontiff. Frederick sought to exploit the situation by the capture of the College of Cardinals but managed to hold only two of them. For a time there was peace again, thanks to the mediation of the saintly French king Louis IX, but when a new pope, Innocent IV, had been elected, the contest between Papacy and Empire broke out again. It continued until the emperor's death in 1250, ending a life punctuated with alternate quarrels and favors for his children, legitimate and illegitimate. At the end Frederick made his peace with the Church and was buried in the cathedral at Palermo.

A French pope, Urban IV, in 1264 ordered the celebration throughout the Church of the newly instituted feast of Corpus Christi. This festival, so outstanding a feature in the devotional life of subsequent ages, had its origin in the devotion to the Eucharist of a Cistercian prioress in Liége, who was directed in a vision to seek approval of this method of honoring the Blessed Sacrament. St. Juliana of Mont Cornillon, the Cistercian nun, had the happiness of seeing the feast ordered by her bishop for his diocese, but it was not until the archdeacon of Liége became Pope Urban IV that it was extended to the whole Church.

The death of Frederick II was not the end of the quarrel between pope and emperor. Frederick's heirs carried on the struggle until the Hohenstaufen line came to an end when Charles of Anjou, ruler of Sicily, beheaded Frederick's grandson Conradin in 1268. Clement IV was then on the papal throne, a worthy occupant of it in his opposition to nepotism in ecclesiastical life. We know also that he gave his patronage to the English Franciscan Roger Bacon, the versatile friar with scientific interests who had much trouble with his religious superiors, caused partly by his own pugnacity and partly by their suspicion that the friar's experiments had something to do with witchcraft.

The year following the institution of the feast of Corpus Christi, for which St. Thomas Aquinas had composed the breviary office, was that of the birth of Dante Alighieri in Florence, another addition to the galaxy of poets, philosophers, and mystics that gives so special a savor to the thirteenth century in the annals of the Christian Church. His *Divine Comedy*, the first great poetical work in Italian, is a synthesis of the whole Catholic philosophy of life.

Another interregnum, of three years this time, began in 1268, when Clement IV died; Gregory X became pope in 1271, achieving much in his five years of rule. Abuses in clerical life were swept away and rules were made to safeguard future papal elections. At the second Council of Lyons, convened in 1274, the breach with the Eastern Orthodox Church was ended, though only temporarily. Gregory, himself a churchman of great holiness (beatified by Clement XI in 1713), bade two saints attend the Council of Lyons. They were both friars, mystics, and theologians, St. Thomas Aquinas and St. Bonaventure. It is interesting to record that, despite all they had in common, they did not agree in favoring the then novel vogue for Aristotle, St. Thomas being for, St. Bonaventure against the Greek philosopher.

4. The writings of St. Thomas Aquinas mark the pinnacle of achievement in the intellectual life of the Middle Ages. His work as philosopher and theologian, moreover, is more than a historical monument. It has influenced Catholic thought during all the centuries since Aquinas's time, and it is a fair inference from Leo XIII's encyclical *Aeterni Patris* (1879) that the Thomist philosophy will henceforth remain the formative element in philosophical work within the Church. Neither Aristotle nor St. Thomas, who adapted his thought to the uses of Christian philosophy and theology, was accepted without strife. In fact, there were zealous and learned churchmen who regarded the Angelic Doctor and his disciples as little better than heretics. It must be remembered, in order to understand this attitude, that the translations in use at the time were chiefly those of Avicenna and Averroes, both Mohammedans. Averroes (1126-1198) was particularly obnoxious and had given his name to a school of thought, Averroism, leading in one direction to rationalism and in another to a pantheistic mysticism. One archbishop of Paris condemned these translations of the Greek thinker, but St. Thomas, thanks to learned fellow Dominicans, had access to accurate Latin versions made directly from the Greek texts.

The life of the big, corpulent friar, of calm, sunny, perhaps rather phlegmatic temperament, nicknamed the "Dumb Ox" by his fellow students when he was a youth, was slightly less than fifty years. The sheer volume of the work he did in his span of life is astounding, especially when we take into account that he was a friar giving long hours to the communal singing of the Divine Office in choir and spending hours in mystical contemplation in church or in the privacy of his cell.

His greatest contributions to Christian intellectual life are his two major works, the *Summa contra Gentiles,* a treatise on God as the object of philosophy, that is to say, of the human mind guided by the light of reason, and the great *Summa Theologica,* still incomplete at the time of his death and finished by other theologians of the Dominican order. St. Thomas's two *Summas* contain the most profound synthesis of thought about God, first as known by the human mind as a purely "natural" instrument and, in the second case, by the mind aided by revelation. St. Thomas was poet and mystic as well as what our age calls an intellectual. The evidence is in the Eucharistic hymns written for the office of Corpus Christi and in the most beautiful of all Eucharistic prayers, *Adoro Te devote* ("Hidden God, devoutly I adore Thee"), appearing in the Roman Missal.

This great Dominican's death was in keeping with the whole tenor of his life; it took place while he was about his Father's business. He was teaching at Naples as the Council of Lyons was being convened, and the pope bade him attend. Obediently he set forth on the arduous journey northwards, but he was taken ill on the way to Rome and had to ask hospitality at the Cistercian house at

Fossanuova. The monks took him in and nursed him, but he died on March 7, 1274. With his passing we are near the close of the most brilliant portion of the stretch of time we call the Middle Ages.

9. The Church in the Middle Ages:

St. Catherine of Siena

1. The Church, a living organism, has periods of sickness and decline alternating with spiritual health and well-being. With the deaths of St. Thomas Aquinas (1274), St. Bonaventure a few months later and, two years afterwards, the saintly Pope Gregory X, who had summoned them to the second Council of Lyons, we see the close of one of the happier periods; it is also the end of the medieval dream of "the two swords," the spiritual power of the Papacy and the military power of the Holy Roman Empire wielded in support of the See of Peter. In slightly under two and a half centuries began the movement in Germany that grew into the Protestant Reformation.

Within the sixteen years after the death of Blessed Gregory X six popes occupied the papal throne. They were not bad popes. They were conscientious churchmen, several of them scholars, and one of them a pontiff of outstanding holiness of life (Innocent V, beatified by Leo XIII in 1898). When the last of these popes died in 1292, there was another of those intervals, two years in this case, of a headless Church. Then occurred one of the strangest incidents in papal history.

A conclave, of eleven cardinals only, was convened to elect a new pope but was forced to leave Rome on account of one of those violent feuds between rival families, the Colonnas and the Orsinis. Unfortunately the cardinals carried the partisan spirit with them to the Umbrian hill town of Perugia. They kept up an ecclesiastical war of invective and intrigue, and their ballots were hopelessly split. At length a majority agreed on a course of action. The summer heats had worn them down and the mounting anger of the populace frightened them; moreover, the medieval reverence for sanctity influenced even these quarrelsome dignitaries. They had heard of a holy man, one Peter Morone, living as a hermit with a few other monks on a mountain in the Abruzzi. He was eighty years old, of peasant stock and, although a monk and a priest, no paragon of learning. Still, he was reputed a saint, so in July the cardinals sent a deputation to fetch him, so that they might place him on the papal throne.

Statecraft was unknown to him and in Rome he improvised a hermit's cell for himself in the papal quarters. The energetic and strong-willed Cardinal Gaetano, who had opposed the hermit's election, managed affairs. By the beginning of Advent the new pope, Celestine V, decided to abdicate. Cardinal Gaetano was accused of bringing this about. He protested his innocence, but he was elected pope when Celestine had abdicated. The old hermit wished to go back to his mountain, but he had to be content with a retreat in a castle, for Pope Boniface VIII was not going to risk anyone's using the old monk as a puppet. Peter died two years later. Dante put him in the Inferno for making *il gran rifiuto* ("the great refusal"), but Clement V canonized him in 1313. The incident is the beginning of an era of decline in the authority of the Papacy.

2. We see the weakened state of the Papacy in Boniface VIII's stormy pontificate. His troubles no longer came from imperial ambitions of the Holy Roman, actually German, emperor, but from French nationalism embodied in King Philip IV, *Le Bel* ("the Fair"). The pope's two famous Bulls, *Unam Sanctam,* asserting the papal prerogatives, and *Clericis laicos,* condemning secular taxation of the clergy, are in the spirit of St. Gregory VII, but there was no Canossa this time. The French king resorted to calumny and violence. He accused the pope of heresy, talked of a Council to "depose" him, and sent the royal vice-chancellor with troops to arrest him. At Anagni the French behaved abominably, even assaulting the elderly pontiff. Ironically, he was in greater peril from his own countrymen, the Italian Colonnas, than from the French. The local citizens rescued him from both, and, a sick and broken man, he went back to Rome; there the Orsinis, enemies of the Colonnas, "protected" him, but it was in reality a protective custody. Boniface died shortly after (October 1303).

This unhappy pope was succeeded by a conciliatory and diplomatic Dominican who became Benedict XI. He did much to improve relations with his predecessor's ene- mies, but without giving way on matters of principle. It was unfortunate for the Church that he survived his election by a year only; his accession had seemed to give sound hope of better times ahead. After his death, things took a turn for the worse.

Clement V, elected in 1305, had been archbishop of Bordeaux and he was in favor with the troublesome King Philip IV. Pope Clement was a good deal of an opportunist and ready to help out a large crowd of needy and greedy relatives. He reversed the "strong" policy of his predecessors and, although he stood out against the king's wish to assemble a Council as superior to the pope, he was a party to the unjust and cruel suppression of the Knights-Templars. The king sought to get his hands on some of the wealth of the order. They had, it is true, become over-rich for men vowed to poverty and had gone in for a good deal of financial activity at odds with their religious vocation. That, apparently, was all, but they were charged with all manner of abominations, including witchcraft, homosexuality, and extortionate usury. They were harried and tortured and their Grand Master and his deputy were burned at the stake. Of their wealth the king grabbed a part and some was given to the Knights Hospitalers, another military order, whose special work, however, was not fighting, but the care of sick, infirm, and injured pilgrims.

Pope Clement, a Gascon by birth, disliked the prospect of living in Rome, notorious for its fevers and its turbulent citizenry. Some time after his coronation, which took place at Lyons, he moved to Avignon and stayed there for the rest of his life. Thus began the so-called "Babylonian captivity," a seventy-year span when the popes lived in France and left the papal city in the hands of subordinates to deal as best they could with incessant violence. Clement probably wished to substitute Avignon for Rome as the permanent residence of the popes. After nine years as pontiff he had created two dozen cardinals, twenty-three of them French. His successor, elected in 1314, was John XXII, a subject of much controversy in his lifetime and since. He was an energetic administrator, with a gift for financial organization. There was a good deal of unrest in his time, some of it caused by the excessive zeal of a section of the Franciscan order, rigorists with strange visions of a new—and generally antipapal—revival of primitive Christianity, including an extreme form of religious poverty among the Friars-Minor themselves. This was complicated by a body of agitators demanding a Council that would exert authority over the pope. Support was given to these movements by the English Franciscan called, after his native village south of London, William of Ockham. It is significant that in matters of philosophy his special trait, a distrust of human reason and the value of ordinary logic, was much esteemed by the Protestant Reformers, Luther proclaiming himself an "Occamist."

As the fourteenth century ran its course, various disruptive tendencies gathered followers. In England a priest named John Wyclif had collected a body of earnest disciples, itinerant priests who set an example of poverty and zeal but whose preaching came to include doctrines that attacked the objective nature of sacraments and undermined church authority. Wyclif himself was never molested and died peacefully in his rectory in England, but his ideas had been taken up by John Huss in Bohemia, who died at the stake as a heretic. The so-called "spirituals" among the Franciscans, also known, perhaps with sarcastic intent at first, as the *fraticelli* or little brothers, lent themselves to the general unrest by supporting Louis of Bavaria, seeking to grasp imperial power and setting up an antipope in Rome. The Romans soon tired of Louis's puppet, drove him out of the city with a shower of stones, and left him no alternative but to go to Avignon and make his peace with John XXII, who appears to have treated him mildly enough and allowed him to spend the rest of his life in Avignon, in nominal captivity.

There was for a time hope of a new understanding between the Papacy and the Eastern Orthodox schismatics when a genuinely earnest and ascetic pope was installed. This was a French Cistercian, Jacques Fournier, who became Pope Benedict XII, a reformer of monastic life, a stern opponent of nepotism. He is credited with a wish to restore the Papacy to Rome, but his successor, Clement VI, a cultivated but worldly patron of the arts, was opposed to such a move, understandably, as the revolt of Cola di Rienzi had just taken place. Rienzi, subject of an opera by Wagner and a novel by the English writer Bulwer Lytton, was a demagogue dreaming of a restoration of the glory that was Rome. He set himself up as "tribune of the Roman Republic," under special guidance of the Holy Spirit. He won popularity as a reformer and a friend of the oppressed. In the end his sense of power made him arrogant; he offended the Romans and was murdered.

This strange interlude of revolt and dictatorship with mystical undertones deferred hopes of an early return of the popes from Avignon. The year of Rienzi's revolt (1347), however, was that in which was born the saint who would be instrumental in bringing the last of the Avignon popes back to Rome.

An idea, derived perhaps from Luther's later wild talk about the "Babylonian captivity," often deceived men into seeing the Avignon popes as merely a succession of worldly churchmen, given to nepotism, luxury, avarice, and a degraded subservience to the French crown. It is worth while taking note of the saintly pontiff who was enthroned in Avignon in the middle of the fourteenth century. Urban V (beatified in 1870) was a Benedictine monk before his promotion to high office, and all his life thereafter he displayed the humility and asceticism of a monk. A friend to education, he was active in promoting centers of learning, including several universities and the famous medical school of Montpellier. As a lover of peace he sent the able Cardinal Albornoz to Italy to deal with the turbulence and disorder rampant there, and he tried in vain to bring an end to the wasteful and futile Hundred Years' War between France and England. He, like Benedict XII, wished to reestablish the Papacy in Rome. The majority of his cardinals, fellow Frenchmen, were strongly opposed to this, but Urban listened to the urgings of the emperor, Charles IV, and the poet Petrarch and made the journey to Rome, preparing to settle his court there. Unhappily the death of the masterful Cardinal Albornoz was the signal for new and more formidable outbreaks of violence. This, and his preoccupation with the war between France and England, led him to return to Avignon in 1370 and there he died a few months later.

The Christendom of St. Francis, St. Dominic, and St. Thomas Aquinas presented a tragic picture in the closing decades of the fourteenth century. The Papacy had been weakened by its long struggle, first with the empire, then with the French monarchy, and its prestige had suffered by the removal to Avignon. Worst misfortune for western civilization and for the Church was the Black Death, which swept over Europe with an appalling mortality for two and a half years in the middle of the century. Estimates of the number of deaths from the disease, a form of bubonic plague, vary; it is probable that at least a third of Europe's population was lost. In certain areas the percentage of deaths was higher; it is thought that a half of England's population was wiped out. The effect on the Church was disastrous. Religious communities were decimated or, very often, entirely destroyed; parishes were left without their clergy, for the death rate among the secular priests, living in the towns and villages where the pestilence raged, was disproportionately high. When something like normal life could be resumed, ill-educated and often unworthy candidates were hastily ordained by desperate bishops and put in charge of parishes.

3. The last of the Avignon popes was Pierre Roger de Beaufort, who became Gregory XI. The ending of this phase of papal history brings us face to face with one of the most remarkable and almost certainly the most admirable figure of the fourteenth century. On the whole it is a depressing period to contemplate. St. Catherine of Siena (1347-1380) stands out, calling forth our respect for her sanctity and compelling our affection by the charm of

her personality, against a background of the world's evil and stupidity.

Catherine Benincasa was one of an enormous brood of children born into a petty bourgeois family in the Fontebranda, an industrial quarter of medieval Siena, malodorous with the fumes from the tanners' and dyers' yards. Catherine was precocious in understanding and in piety. Her education was of the skimpiest. We know she mastered the art of reading in adult years, but it is doubtful she ever learned to write. The famous letters and her mystical treatises were all dictated. In spite of mystical gifts—ecstatic prayer, visions, the stigmata—she was a practical young woman. When she joined the Mantellate or Dominican tertiaries it was very largely for taking part in the tasks of a social worker.

When she was in her twenties her visions, like the voices of St. Joan of Arc over a century later, called on her for a special mission, to call the pope back to Rome. Another remarkable woman of the period, St. Bridget of Sweden (or Birgitta), had written letters to the pontiff to urge the return to Rome, but Catherine made the long and toilsome journey to France to present her case in person. Gregory was impressed by the character of the young Dominican tertiary from Italy, but he was a hesitant man, averse from firm decisions. St. Catherine had a strong will; she did not leave Avignon until she had extracted a promise from the pope, whereupon she went back to Siena and her life of good works, penance, and mystical prayer. She would not let the pontiff forget his promise; she dictated two letters to him, addressing him as *Babbo mio* ("Dear Grandpa"), a form of address she used also for his successor.

Gregory XI returned to Rome but did not long survive his voyage. In the spring of 1378 there was an election so beset with violence and terrorism that its validity could be questioned. This led to the calamitous period of the

Great Schism, forty years when two and at times three claimants to the Papacy competed for the allegiance of Catholics.

The cardinals who assembled after Gregory's death held their conclave in fear of their lives from the rioting mob that demanded an Italian pope. Hastily the voters, although mostly Frenchmen, produced a majority ballot for Archbishop Prignano of Bari, who immediately took the title of Urban VI and received the traditional homage of the few Italian dignitaries present. The French cardinals now swore the election had been "rigged," retired in anger to a provincial town, and elected Robert of Geneva, a cardinal with a reputation for cruelty in putting down a rebellion. He set up his court in Avignon, taking the title of Clement VII. Thus began the Great Schism of the west, a tragic quarrel with no doctrine at stake but destined to destroy all hope of restoring the spiritual unity of the west and, as subsequent ages could see, paving the way for the great upheaval of the sixteenth century.

Pope Urban VI was an unfortunate man. He was virtuous, earnest, and zealous for reform, appreciative, too, of sanctity as he met it in the remarkable young woman who had done so much to bring the Papacy back to Rome. He suffered from the defects of his own qualities. His reforming zeal became a harsh tyranny and he alienated even the cardinals who had been his supporters against the French faction. St. Catherine dictated letters urging him to moderate the harshness of his dealings with others. To the end of her short life of thirty-three years she was convinced of the validity of Urban's election.

The conflicting claims of popes and antipopes and the division of the Catholic world into two mutually hostile camps strengthened the erroneous belief in the overriding authority of a general council. This in part explains the attitude of the "Council" of Pisa, which met in 1409.

This assemblage was called together neither by the validly elected pope, Gregory XII, nor by the antipope who called himself Benedict XIII, but by cardinals attached to both pope and antipope. It proceeded to condemn as schismatics and usurpers both Gregory and Benedict, the Peter de Luna who had at first supported Urban VI. It then elected a Greek cardinal who took the title of Alexander V, so that now three rivals claimed the allegiance of Catholics.

These four decades of feud, scandal, and confusion were ended in 1417, in as strange a manner as the thing had begun. The Council of Constance met in the German town which gives it its name in 1415. It had been called together by the adventurer Baldassare Cossa, self-styled John XXIII. Gregory XII in Rome, not having convened it, did not recognize it, but two years later he changed his mind and did so. This gave it ecumenical status. John XXIII took fright, tried to flee, and set up another "Council," but the emperor Sigismund had him arrested, tried for simony, and deposed, a decision which Cossa made up his mind to accept. Old Pope Gregory XII, nearing ninety, chose to abdicate, in the interests of peace and unity. In the winter of 1417 the cardinals met in conclave and elected Oddone (Odo) Colonna. As it was the feast of St. Martin he took the title of Martin V. The Great Schism of the west was ended. There was general rejoicing, except in the case of the obdurate Peter de Luna ("Benedict XIII") and a handful of irreconcilables who had taken refuge in Spain.

10. The Church in the Renaissance

1. The term *renaissance,* literally a rebirth, has been used of various periods in history. We have seen it applied to the revival of Christian culture in Europe after the Dark Ages, maturing in the twelfth century and reaching its highest point in the thirteenth. That was a renaissance essentially Christian.

Now we have to see the Church in the period called the Renaissance without further qualification. It is a movement that was coming to its birth as the western world was once more emerging from a time of transition and decline, the fourteenth century, which a modern Dutch historian, J. Huizinga, has called the waning of the Middle Ages. Scholastic philosophy was becoming bogged down in hairsplitting and subtlety for its own sake. The Papacy had been weakened by the Avignon interlude and the Great Schism. The rationalism of the great Scholastics was being replaced by an appeal to emotional and intuitive attitudes. We notice the disdain for the Schoolmen in the great spiritual classic of the time, *The Imitation of Christ.* The zeal of the Crusaders to regain the holy places in

Palestine was forgotten. Even the fall of Constantinople to the Turks in 1453 failed to reawaken it.

During these years, the later fourteenth and the early fifteenth century, a new ferment was at work in western civilization. This was the rediscovery and the renewed appreciation of the classical cultures of Greece and Rome. Perhaps the best representative of the early phase of the Renaissance is the Italian poet Petrarch (1304-1374), who has been described as the first modern man. The movement had its first flowering in the Mediterranean countries and then made its way northward.

The subject matter of this revival was pagan in origin, the Greek and the classical Latin languages and the masterpieces written in them. Aristotle was one of the great pagans, and the Catholic Church assimilated his thought and fused it with her doctrine in the Thomist theology. Why, we may ask, did she not do the same with the later Renaissance? There are two answers to this question. In the first place, she took over the very thought fabric of Aristotle and adapted it to a reasoned exposition of Christian doctrine, as when his philosophy was used in relation to the Real Presence in the Eucharist. The scholars of the classical Renaissance, on the other hand, seized with enthusiasm on the languages, the outward forms, and literary arts of the ancient world and made little or no effort to weld pagan culture with Christian doctrine. The second reason for the partial failure of the later Renaissance to merge with Christian belief and practice is the character of the men who ruled the Church at the time. That is not to say that the popes in the century between the end of the Great Schism (1417) and the first rumblings of the Protestant Reformation (1517) were "bad" popes. There was one whose life gave scandal; others were good and even zealous churchmen, but they did not command the respect, even the reluctant respect, given to a Hildebrand or an Innocent III. As tem-

poral rulers they competed with other temporal rulers at
their own level. If they failed, the Papacy lost prestige; if
they succeeded, their action was resented. They were in
a quandary. The spread of the "conciliar" heresy* forced
them to resort to political and often to military action to
keep their independence. The pope who refused to be a
sovereign would find he had become someone's subject.

A papal election in the middle of the fifteenth century,
only a few years before Constantinople fell, put on the
papal throne a pope who was scholar and statesman and a
friend to the new enthusiasm for classical learning or
"humanism," as it was called. Nicholas V, elected in 1447,
gave generously to libraries and to individual scholars. He
paid to have Homer translated into Latin, for Greek was
still an accomplishment of few, even among scholars. One
of his beneficiaries was Lorenzo Valla, the best Latinist
of his time and one of the few who were versed in classical
Greek; he translated Thucydides and Herodotus into
Latin.

It is an error to picture the decades before the Reformation as spiritually moribund, with all energy and enthusiasm diverted to the new learning. There was a rich development of spiritual life in northern Europe, especially
among the Brethren of the Common Life, founded late
in the fourteenth century by Gerard Groote, a Dutch
religious who was friendly with the Flemish mystic John
Ruysbroeck. Somewhat later appear two great Franciscan
saints, bound by personal friendship and by their work in
the Observant reform of the order. St. Bernardine and
St. John Capistrano were both eminent preachers, the
first as the propagator of the new devotion to the Holy
Name of Jesus, the second as a defender of orthodox
teaching in regions where the Hussite errors were gaining

* The conciliar "theory" or heresy taught that the authority of a general
council was superior to that of the pope, whose decisions, therefore, could
be overruled by those of the assembled bishops of the Church.

adherents. St. John Capistrano, then a man of seventy, went to Belgrade to encourage the troops who were defending it against Turkish attack. Crucifix in hand, he led the left wing of the forces under the Hungarian patriot Hunyadi.

The Moslem peril, after the fall of the Byzantine empire in midcentury (1453), was the preoccupation of the Spanish pope Calixtus III, but his efforts to stir up enthusiasm for a new Crusade were in vain. This pope was, despite his zeal for saving Christendom from the Turks, singularly careless of the best interests of the Church when it was a matter of bestowing favors. Calixtus, a Borja (Borgia) by birth, gave the cardinal's hat to his young nephew Rodrigo, a brilliant but loose-living cleric not yet in priest's orders, a Borgia on his mother's side, who then took the family name of his benefactor.

With the Italian cardinal Piccolomini, who liked to use his first names Latinized as Aeneas Silvius, on the papal throne as Pius II (1458),* the tide of humanism was in full spate. As a student and a minor cleric he had been an ardent devotee of the classics, and when he became pope all the humanists who hoped for favors or lucrative appointments gathered round him. They were disappointed. Pius II, whose life before he took subdeacon's orders had been careless and immoral, now showed himself an earnest churchman. The restoration of classical Latinity and good Greek took second place to the needs of religion, and a false quantity or a misplaced accent in a Greek text, formerly a matter of importance, was forgotten when he contemplated the Mohammedan threat to the western world and the Catholic Church. This was the subject always in his mind throughout his pontificate. So

* A story current at the time of the election asserted that Cardinal Piccolomini, enthusiastic Latinist, chose the name *Pius* less on account of the first pope of that name, St. Pius I of the second century, than in memory of another Aeneas, the *pius Aeneas* of Virgil.

strongly did it possess his heart and mind that at the end of his six years' reign he died in its defense. Despairing of winning the interest and support of worldly rulers by exhortation or the bestowal of spiritual favors, he himself "took the cross" and left Rome with the idea of setting out for Palestine. He reached Ancona, the port from which he was to sail, but was struck down by fever and died in the torrid summer heats of 1464. It is symptomatic of the confusion in the mind of Christendom in the half century or so before the Protestant revolt that Pius, when he had amended his morals and become a conscientious ecclesiastic, was a loyal adherent of the antipope who called himself Felix V, a former Duke of Savoy. Pius, moreover, at that time appears to have believed sincerely in the conciliar theory. That he looked back with remorse on his own early life is apparent in the severe but paternal rebuke he gave the young Borgia cardinal who was destined to become Pope Alexander VI.

In 1459 the citizens of Florence were mourning the death of their archbishop, St. Antoninus, a Dominican friar who had been commanded under religious obedience to accept a prelacy. His sanctity and learning had won his people's respect and affection. He occupies an important place in the intellectual life of the Church for his pioneer work in ethics and economics. His book *Summa moralis* set the pattern for the systematic manuals of moral theology used to guide priests in the work of the confessional. As a Christian economist he offered special guidance for the ethical conduct of business at a time when this was much needed on account of the rapid extension of banking and commerce in Renaissance Italy.

During this time of enthusiasm for the ancient world, its literature, its languages, and its art forms, the outward aspect of the papal city benefited by the encouragement given to art and architecture by the pontiffs. In some cases, that of the old Roman temple of the gods, the Pantheon, for instance, the buildings of imperial Rome were adapted with little change to Christian uses. When new buildings, both ecclesiastical and secular, were designed, the old Roman models were followed and developed into the baroque architecture which at its best is admirable. In the case of churches, so closely was the classical pattern adhered to that the very name of a Roman city hall or town hall, *basilica,* became the accepted term for a large church building, such as the old Lateran church or St. Peter's itself.

Of the abuses which partly explain the violent outbreak of revolt in the early sixteenth century, one of the worst was the amount of nepotism in high ecclesiastical circles, including the Papacy, and the greed of churchmen seeking to enrich themselves and their families. Apart from the scandal given to the laity, this practice had the effect of establishing a vested interest in high offices in the Church, which in turn led to unsuitable men being put into responsible positions. Even a zealous and able pontiff like Sixtus IV, a Franciscan devoted to his order, was guilty of this abuse of his power. This involved him in various quarrels, especially with the wealthy and ambitious Medicis of Florence. The murder of one of the Medicis brought the pope's own nephew under suspicion, and a two-year feud, which included the placing of Florence under an interdict,* was ended only by Sixtus' own diplomacy.

In dealing with the Spanish monarchy, Sixtus displayed a humane spirit only too rare in that violent era. A special Inquisition had been set up in Spain and, under royal control, had rapidly gone beyond what Rome regarded as its lawful authority. Even tough-minded Renaissance

* A punishment inflicted by the Church, especially in the Middle Ages, on a corporate body, such as a city, province, or nation, forbidding public worship, Christian burial, and the administration of the sacraments, except baptism.

Italians were shocked by its ruthlessness; again and again the pope protested and addressed rebukes to the Spanish authorities—in vain. Large numbers of Jews and the *maraños* or nominal proselytes embracing Christianity to escape death at the stake fled to the papal dominions and were allowed to live in a ghetto in Rome. This cannot have provided ideal conditions for them, but at least they were protected by the pope from torture and death by fire and could worship in their own way among themselves.

2. The Papacy of the Renaissance era is considered to have reached its lowest point of worldliness and corruption with the election in 1492 of Rodrigo Borgia to the See of Peter. Cardinal Borgia was the brilliant but loose-living nephew of Calixtus III and had received the red hat at the age of twenty-five. His election was almost certainly a simoniacal one, large bribes being handed out to buy votes in the conclave. So much legend, most of it without even a foundation in recorded fact, has gathered about the name of Alexander VI that some assessment of his pontificate is needed. To his credit we note that he was an able administrator.

One of the earliest events in his reign was the discovery —by an Italian, Columbus, under Spanish patronage—of America. At once the question arose of the claims to newly discovered lands that would be made by the two great sea powers of the age, Spain and Portugal. The pope settled this by the so-called Bull of Demarcation, awarding new territory in the west to Spain, in the east to Portugal. The matter of Alexander's sexual morals, so much canvassed by writers looking for a sensational theme, is a topic that needs unemotional treatment based on known fact. To present the second Borgia pope as a kind of ecclesiastical Bluebeard and his illegitimate son and daughter as paragons of iniquity is entirely unjustified by history. It would seem that Rodrigo Borgia was a typical man of the Renaissance who simply had no kind of "vocation" but possessed the qualities that would have made an efficient and, by the standards of his time, remarkably humane ruler and, be it noted, deeply affectionate lover and father. Perhaps his daughter Lucrezia has suffered more unjustly than her father. His vices have been exaggerated; those attributed to his daughter did not exist. The seductive, adulterous, and murderous *femme fatale* is a myth of fiction and grand opera. Alexander's daughter, born a dozen years before his election to the Papacy, was, indeed, beautiful and her contemporaries have paid tribute to her charm. She was thrice married but met with much unhappiness. Her first marriage was annulled,* her second, a genuine love match, ended in the murder of her husband by his enemies. The third marriage, less tragic, was blighted by her husband's excessive jealousy. She was kind-hearted always, devout, and cultivated.

In the latter part of Alexander VI's pontificate the Dominican friar Girolamo Savonarola was waging his campaign in Florence, one justified by the corruption in Florentine social life, but harsh, puritanical, and undiscriminating in spirit. Moreover, it was antipapal, for the friar, who had been influenced by the conciliar theory, was guilty of intriguing with the French king against the pope. One of Alexander's diplomatic successes had been to effect a balance of power between Spanish and French ambitions so that the Papacy and Italy as a whole were protected against aggression from both rivals. When, finally, the friar was condemned and executed (1498), he was not, as is so often believed, burned at the stake; he was hanged and his dead body was burned. He died, indeed,

* A marriage may be annulled by the Church if it is found that not all the conditions for a valid marriage existed in the first place, hence there was not a true marriage.

with pathetic fortitude and piety, but it is false to repre-sent him as a martyr for the Christian faith.

When Alexander VI died in 1503 he was remembered chiefly for the evil in his life. The good that should have remained in memory was, for a long time, interred with his bones. He was a competent ruler, more just and hu-mane than most, a patron of learning, and a pontiff who gave encouragement to devout brotherhoods for foster-ing pious and charitable work by laymen.

The Borgia pope was followed by an archbishop of Siena who, had his life been prolonged, might have been the reformer whose efforts could have saved a weakened Christendom from dismemberment in the next genera-tion. He was a Piccolomini by adoption, a nephew of Pius II, and a determined opponent of Alexander VI. Un-happily for the Church that needed such a man, he died, as Pius III, within a month of the election.

The last two popes who ruled the See of Peter before a genuine purification of the Church took place were not in any sense bad men. The first of them, Julius II, was a soldier and a statesman, sixty years old when elected but of immense physical and mental energy. He was war-like, stern, and irascible, but withal a patron of the arts, in this a true man of the Renaissance but with a foreshad-owing of things to come in his opposition to nepotism and his reformation of monastic life. He was, too, a zeal-ous supporter of foreign missions. As a patron of the arts he befriended Michelangelo, Raphael, and Bramante, and he laid the foundation stone of the new St. Peter's Church.

Two things were very much in Julius II's mind in the last years of his life; reformation within the Church and action to deal with the Mohammedan threat from without. In 1511 he convened a Council, which assembled the following year as the fifth Lateran Council. The Ro-man fever, which has claimed so many victims until modern times, cut off Julius a few months after the Council assembled, and it was left to resume its sittings under the next pontiff. This was Cardinal Giovanni de'Medici, a son of Lorenzo the Magnificent. He had been destined for an ecclesiastical career—for purely worldly motives— from childhood. He received the tonsure at the age of seven and was made a cardinal when he was about fourteen. Nevertheless, he was not yet in priest's orders when, at the age of thirty-eight, he became pope as Leo X.

Leo's pontificate of eight years closes an era in the history of the Catholic Church. When he ascended the papal throne the Christendom of the Middle Ages still survived, even if weak and with an uncertain tenure of life. When he died the storm had already broken over Germany, and the Christian world was in process of being set in the pattern it still holds—two great bodies of believers we call Catholics (or Roman Catholics) and Protestants. The schismatic eastern Christians who make up the various more or less independent "Orthodox" churches remained unchanged, close to Rome in doctrine and religious practice but with an old legacy of suspicion and dislike.

Leo X, a good-living cleric, strict with himself about such things as fasting and the specific priestly obligations of his state in life, was a true man of the Renaissance in his classical culture, his taste for the arts, and his fondness for associating with artists and men of letters. Perhaps his greatest ambition was to see Rome the acknowledged center of European culture, and in this he was successful. He kept up Julius II's encouragement of Raphael's painting and of Bramante's work on the new St. Peter's. He bestowed a papal secretariat and the cardinal's hat on the humanist scholar Bembo. Also, he promoted Greek studies in the Roman University. In diplomacy and foreign politics he was less of a success than the warlike and strong-willed Julius and was forced to accept humiliating terms for a concordat with France after his forces had suffered a crushing defeat.

The outstanding event in the eight years' rule of Leo X is, of course, the outbreak of the Protestant Reformation. It is clear that he did not grasp the seriousness of what was taking place in the north of Europe or suspect that, for the Church and the whole western world of his time, a volcano was about to burst forth. The first news of disorder to reach Rome, late in 1517, was that an Augustinian priest, one Dr. Martin Luther, was squabbling with the Dominican Tetzel, who had been appointed to campaign in Germany for funds to pay for the work on St. Peter's. Tetzel was authorized to offer a plenary indulgence to all who, complying with the usual conditions— confession and communion—gave an alms according to their means for this work. Dr. Luther had attacked Tetzel for his methods, then gone further and posted a set of theses, dealing with the doctrine of indulgences, on a church door. The theses were also printed and distributed. Tetzel was much incommoded in his task, and the flow of funds for St. Peter's began to shrink.

Leo, the fastidious scholar and lover of the arts, is said to have shrugged off the whole affair as an unseemly brawl of two German—and, therefore, presumably barbarous— friars; a certain acrimonious rivalry between Augustinians and Dominicans often showed itself. Leo X sent orders to the Augustinian vicar-general to silence his troublesome subject, but it was soon learned that Luther had fled beyond the reach of his religious superiors. Less than a year before his death in 1521 Leo excommunicated Luther, now openly a rebel. Shortly after this the pope gave the title of *Fidei Defensor* (Defender of the Faith) to King Henry VIII of England for his book in defense of the seven sacraments against Luther's teaching on the subject.

When Leo died, the Protestant revolt was gaining momentum rapidly. Devout Catholics, clerical and lay, had long desired a reformation "in head and members" within the Church. Now the initiative had been seized by men ready, as Goethe put it, to tear asunder the seamless robe of Christ.

11. The Church and the Protestant Reformation

1. A few words about the terms we use are desirable as preliminary to a survey of the two great movements called the Protestant Reformation (or simply the Reformation) and the Counter Reformation. Whether one likes or dislikes the first of these things and what came out of it, logic compels one to admit that the willed destruction of an institution as it exists and the substitution of other ideas for its basic beliefs is more than a *reformation;* it is a revolution, a revolt against it. Usage has accustomed us to the term "Protestant Reformation" for the sixteenth-century Lutheran movement and its kindred developments in England, Scotland, Switzerland, and other countries, so the label may be accepted as convenient.

One can easily oversimplify the beginnings of the Protestant Reformation. A few salient facts, however, stand out as partial causes of its early success. The Avignon exile of the popes, the Great Schism, the widespread acceptance of the conciliar theory, and the amount of nepotism and acquisitiveness in the higher ranks of the clergy had unsettled many minds and predisposed them to rebellion. We may add to all this the scandal given by the personal life of the second Borgia pope, Alexander VI, although the effect of this has been exaggerated, so firmly rooted in the pre-Reformation Catholic mind was the distinction between the sanctity of a man's office, as priest, bishop, or pope, and his personal worthiness.

Then there was the scandal of the money-raising for St. Peter's when Leo X had become pope. In this case the word "scandal" applies rather to incidental abuses of subordinate church officials and their effect on men's minds than to any wrongdoing by the pope. Leo X was not guilty of malpractice. He was ill-informed about conditions in the north and he was ill-served by those appointed to work for him. He was, however, party to an arrangement that looks like cynical opportunism on behalf of the ecclesiastical cause he had at heart.

If we use the metaphor of a train of gunpowder for what led to Luther's revolt, we may say that the spark which fired the train was the pope's desire to finish building St. Peter's. Julius II in 1506 had laid the foundation stone of Bramante's new basilica; it was for Julius's successors to complete the work.

2. Most important of all, as so often at turning points in history, there is *the man*. He may be saint or villain or, more often, something between the two, but he will always be a genius. Such was Martin Luther (1483-1546), whose life of sixty-three years coincides more or less with the transition from the Middle Ages to the modern world. From about 1517 until twenty years later, when Pope Paul III took the first steps towards assembling a council to reform the Catholic Church from within, Martin Luther was the most prominent figure in the western world, a single, impassioned voice raised against the Roman pontiff, whom Luther's world had hitherto recognized as the Vicar of Christ. Estimates of Luther range from the filial piety of village artists in Germany who painted him en-

haloed as a saint to the stern judgment of England's Protestant Dean Inge, who saw him as the spiritual ancestor of Hitler. To grasp what happened in the first half of the sixteenth century and why it happened so quickly we need an objective picture of this remarkable man, so far as it can be separated from legend and biased accounts.

Luther was born in a small Saxon town in 1483. Of his early life we know little, except his humble parentage, his strict upbringing, and his academic success in school and university. His father wished him to become a lawyer, and he entered on postgraduate law studies. When he was twenty years old he gave up the idea of law, much to his father's annoyance. His spiritual Odyssey from this point is interesting and calls for sympathy if it is to be made intelligible. He had resolved to enter monastic life. This was to fulfill a vow made to St. Anne in a moment of peril during a thunderstorm. Accordingly, in 1505 he joined the so-called Hermits of St. Augustine in Erfurt. Actually the order had long ceased to be eremitical and its members were engaged in preaching, theological study, and a great deal of teaching, mostly at the university level.

Luther's life as a novice and a young priest—he had a year's novitiate and was ordained less than a year after that—was not tepid or corrupt, as his enemies asserted later in the heat of controversy. He was ultradevout and he suffered for a long time from intense and continuous scrupulosity. Any experienced director of souls can bear witness to the havoc which this state of indecision and spiritual distress can work on the mind and heart of the victim, so here perhaps we should see a partial explanation of the subsequent career of the pious Augustinian friar who became a great heresiarch. During this trying time his superiors and fellow religious were kind to him and tried to help him, he tells us, but in vain.

While still studying theology the young priest was appointed to lecture on Aristotle in the university of Wittenberg. At this time he paid his first and only visit to Rome. He was sent there on business of his order, or rather of one section of it at odds with another over proposed changes. The papal city of Julius II did two things to the earnest Augustinian priest. It stimulated his emotional piety. He made the customary acts of devotion of pilgrims to Rome, for he was still a believer in holy relics. Secondly, he was repelled and disgusted by the corrupt lives of many of the clergy. This, unhappily, was the stronger impression; "The nearer Rome," he said afterwards, "the worse Christian." At this time he wished that his father and mother were dead so that he might pray them out of Purgatory.

For another four years after the Roman journey Luther was lecturing in the university on various books of the Bible. During this time he developed the concept or, as he claimed, had it revealed to him by the Holy Ghost, of justification by faith. This is the heart of his whole system of theology. He was much troubled in mind about the meaning of the "justice" of God in chapter I, verse 17 of St. Paul's Epistle to the Romans. The Revised Version of the King James Bible uses the word "righteousness," but Luther pondered the Latin *justitia* of the Vulgate. Already he had lost respect for the scholastic theologians. His guide was the English Franciscan, William of Ockham, whose blend of skepticism and fideism—*willed* faith unaided by reason or even opposed to it—appealed strongly to him. Also, he had found, as he thought, confirmation of his own discovery in the writings of St. Augustine.

To summarize the essential point of Luther's doctrine very briefly: by the Fall (the sin of Adam) man's nature was wholly corrupted; here we have the "total depravity" of old-fashioned Puritanism, taught also by Calvin. The human will *of itself* was incapable of an act pleasing to

God, hence the worthlessness of so-called good works. The human will, in fact, was not free; only divine grace, without being earned or merited, could impart any value to man's deeds or give him hope of salvation. The possession of this grace, moreover, did not mean that the soul was changed at all. It had no goodness of itself, but Christ deigned to *impute* to it His own goodness in virtue of His sacrifice on the cross. The logical deductions from these basic ideas are revolutionary. One wonders whether Luther himself grasped their full significance at first and whether his colleagues saw how completely his ideas were at variance with Catholic belief. That the Augustinian professor's lectures were having an effect, we know from his own enthusiastic account of the desertion of scholastic studies and the popularity of "our" theology.

Luther's "revelation" is the true starting point of the Protestant Reformation. The first open clash with church authority was in 1517. Now occurred the controversy about indulgences, constantly quoted but too often misunderstood. At first Luther did not attack the doctrine of indulgences, that is, the authority of the Church to offer, in consideration of works of piety, the remission of the *temporal* punishment for sins repented of, confessed, and pardoned. In the beginning of the affair Luther attacked certain scandalous abuses—and they were certainly glaring enough.

3.   The ecclesiastical gossip of the day centered on Archbishop Albert of Magdeburg, who had authority over the diocese in which Luther was working. This prelate was a younger brother of the Elector of Brandenburg. Albert had been made an archbishop at the age of twenty-two, by papal dispensation. Several years later the archiepiscopal see of Mainz fell vacant and Albert wished to have that as well. For one young archbishop, even of a princely family, to hold two archdioceses at the same

time appeared scandalous. Even an easy-going Medici pontiff hesitated, but there were reasons of state connected with the next election of an emperor. Leo X gave way. He needed money for the work on St. Peter's; the induction of an archbishop carried with it the payment of large fees to the papal court. There had, unfortunately, been several archbishops of Mainz in rather quick succession and the archdiocese had paid the bills. Archbishop Albert, needing to borrow money, went to the house of Fugger. The Fuggers of Augsburg were something like one of the great financial families of the United States. They had interests in various concerns—metals, real estate, overseas trade—and they had a Midas touch in business, but they were not robber barons. They were devoted Catholics and good philanthropists. From them the archbishop had the loan he required.

The method by which he would pay Rome and repay the Fuggers seems to have been worked out without Pope Leo's knowledge, although he accepted it when told of it. To encourage almsgiving for the building of the new St. Peter's he granted a plenary indulgence to all who contributed and met the condition for such an indulgence, which was a valid confession so that the recipient would be in a state of grace; communion was desirable but not essential. The work of publicizing the indulgence and collecting the alms was entrusted to the Dominicans. In charge of the campaign in Germany was one of their order, John Tetzel, a friar who for some years had specialized in this work. Of the money he collected, half would go to Rome for St. Peter's. The other half was the archbishop's and with it he would repay the principal and interest of the Fugger loan.

Father Tetzel's indiscretion was Dr. Luther's opportunity. The Dominican did not, as is sometimes said, sell the indulgence, although he did circulate to bishops and parish priests a tariff of alms that might reasonably be expected of various donors, from the large sum a prince or bishop ought to give down through various economic levels to the widow's mite of the truly poor. There was even a recommendation that the indulgence should not be refused to those who could contribute nothing but their prayers and their good will. This is not shocking in itself. Tetzel erred in his pulpit utterances, especially on the subject of applying the indulgence to the souls in Purgatory. This concept was a relatively new one to Luther's contemporaries. About forty years earlier the pope had first granted such an indulgence, but he had made it clear that not even the Vicar of Christ could guarantee the immediate release from Purgatory of a soul for whom an indulgence was gained. Tetzel, spiritual accountant and statistician, was much more specific—erroneously. Seven years' punishment, here or in Purgatory, was due for each mortal sin that had been forgiven, he said, so the plight of some of the poor souls was a sad one, but let their friends or relatives still on earth gain the plenary indulgence for them and they would forthwith be translated to Paradise. This was bad enough, but it was charged that the friar was guilty of an even worse error—that the indulgence applied to a soul in Purgatory would take effect although the giver of the alms was not in a state of grace.

Wittenberg, All Saints Day (November 1), 1517—such were the place and the time of Luther's first overt act in a drama that ended in the greatest cataclysm that has fallen on the Catholic Church. He wrote out and posted his ninety-five theses on the door of a church wherein his prince, the Elector Frederick III of Saxony, kept a vast collection of relics. The theses, according to the old-time practice of the "schools" of philosophy and theology, were a challenge to all and sundry to debate them with their author. Luther sent copies to various universities and to the archbishop of Mainz. There was no public debate, but Tetzel defended himself in lectures at Frankfort. Then Luther began his preaching campaign against Tetzel and his handling of the pope's indulgence. Until that memorable November 1 of 1517 he had been an earnest Augustinian priest with some authority in his order and a modest local fame. Almost overnight he became the most talked-of man in Germany and soon the whole of Europe was in turmoil because of him. Certain personal traits contributed to his influence. He was deeply emotional, incredibly industrious, and an eloquent speaker and preacher. He was a master of the German language as spoken by the mass of his countrymen, colorful, vigorous, coarse to a degree that requires rows of asterisks when he is translated for modern readers.

The Dominicans complained to the archbishop. The latter passed the complaint to Rome and the pope ordered the vicar-general of the Augustinian Hermits to silence his subject. The Augustinians, however, were mostly sympathetic to their colleague. To John Staupitz, his own superior, Luther said that he "owed everything." The Elector Frederick, too, had become his strong supporter and gladly intervened on his behalf. The Dominicans in Rome pressed for action and the pope ordered Luther to Rome, then, despairing of the friar's obedience, he instructed the papal legate, Cardinal Cajetan (Thomas de Vio), to have him arrested. Elector Frederick stepped in and the order to the cardinal was modified; he was to examine Luther and persuade him to retract if possible. The legate was a priest of deep learning and lofty character; he was also a very human person, of much kindness and vast patience; Luther himself bore witness to this. It was all in vain. Luther would not retract, but he was allowed to depart from the place of conference. This was in the late fall of 1518. A month later he took a momentous step, flouting

Pope Leo X's authority and appealing to a future general Council.

4. In 1519 the Emperor Maximilian died and his grandson was elected to succeed him. The young emperor, Charles V, then in his twentieth year, was competent, strong-willed, a great administrator. He was attached to the Catholic faith, but political motives made him hopeful of a reconciliation with the religious rebels. His great error was to dream that the occupant of the Holy See and these new critics could somehow find a working compromise.

Luther's teaching was solemnly condemned in June 1520 by the papal Bull *Exsurge, Domine.* Luther and his friends were given sixty days wherein to recant. They held a riotous celebration in Wittenberg, in December, burning a copy of the Bull as well as a volume of canon law in a public bonfire.

Young Charles V postponed action in the matter until the Diet (Reichstag or Parliament) met at Worms early in 1521. This was the occasion of Luther's possibly mythical "Here I stand." He did not wait for the Catholic emperor to arrest him. His friend the Saxon Elector staged a "kidnaping" and hid him away in the castle of Wartburg, where he began a war of pamphlets attacking various Catholic doctrines and practices. There was no question now of his having departed from orthodox teaching, although he would continue to maintain that his was the authentic Christian faith, the rest "Popish" corruptions.

In 1522 Leo X was succeeded by the good Dutch pope, Adrian VI. He was a genuinely religious churchman, desirous of reform, and very conscious of the harm done by worldly ecclesiastics. His own reign was too short for him to make headway against the vested interests in nepotism and money-making. He was succeeded by Clement VII, a

Medici cousin of Leo X. As archbishop of Florence he had been respected for virtuous living and devotion to pastoral work, but he was a hesitant ruler, vacillating in policy, and blind to the menace of the Lutheran revolt. His political strategy was disastrous. He opposed Charles V and made an alliance with France. The result was a terrible sack of Rome in 1527, for which the emperor sought to disclaim responsibility. Meanwhile Luther's influence grew rapidly and the whole of Germany was, as one observer put it, "ablaze." The Peasants' Revolt of 1524-1525 in protest against intolerable conditions under serfdom had received Luther's approval at first. Later, when the luckless peasants were defeated in battle and many of them executed, Luther turned against them and urged the victors to slaughter without mercy.

During the time of this affair and the troubles in Rome the religious revolt in Germany had got out of hand. The emperor had been calling for a Council, as had the rebellious Luther. Charles V now voiced the hope of a settlement, a hope shared by Luther's disciple and admirer, the young classical scholar Philip Melanchthon (Schwarzerd). There were to be discussions and a formal statement of the ideas of Luther and his party. The papal representative was Cardinal Campeggio, recently back from his discussions with Henry VIII in London about the king's wish for an annulment of his marriage to Catherine of Aragon.

Late in 1530 the Lutherans issued their manifesto; we know it as the Confession of Augsburg. The orthodox theologians replied with a *Confutatio,* and to that in turn Melanchthon answered with an *Apologia.* Cardinal Campeggio was moderate and conciliatory. He even offered dispensations for a married priesthood and for the laity to receive communion under the two forms of bread and wine; these were demands of the reformers. Melanchthon, the young humanist, was pleased and told his master of the legate's offer; Luther's reply is unprintable. The Prot-estants—the name was in use by this time*—now be-came an organized party of revolt. The princes in sympa-thy with the Lutherans met at Schmalkalden, in Thurin-gia, and banded themselves into a League in 1531.

In the following spring the theological quarrel was put aside temporarily. The Turks, against whom the popes had for generations tried to unite the Christian rulers, were advancing into the heart of Europe. They were on their way up the valley of the Danube. Charles and the Protestant princes agreed on a truce in the summer of 1532, the Interim of Nuremberg. Such was the beginning of Protestantism as part of the fabric of European political life.

5. Two regional developments of the Protestant revolt added to the religious confusion and left many men won-dering about the future of the Christian world. These were, first, the events that plunged Switzerland into reli-gious strife and civil war and, second, the quarrel between the Tudor autocrat Henry VIII and the Papacy, ending the union that had survived for nine centuries since the monk St. Augustine had become the Anglo-Saxons' first archbishop.

The first breakaway from Catholicism in Switzerland took place in Zurich in 1522, the year when the Dutch pope Adrian VI was elected. In Germany the teachers of the new religion had looked to princely rulers for support; in England a king dictated his subjects' religion. There were neither kings nor princes in the Swiss cantons, which formed a federation of separate states jealously guarding their independence. The Protestant movements in the country were guided by two very different leaders, one a

* The word *Protestant* had its origin in the *Protestatio* of the Lutheran princes who objected to the ruling of the Diet of Speyer (1529) against further innovations in religion.

native son, the other a Frenchman domiciled there. For the present we may consider the first of these affairs.

Ulrich Zwingli, one of the numerous children in a well-to-do peasant family, had as uncle a parish priest who interested himself in the boy's education. Ulrich became a priest, probably unwisely, for he was temperamentally unfitted for the life, as was Luther. He was zealous and scholarly, however, and a devotee of Erasmus. After hard work as a parish priest he was appointed to an important post in Zurich. A diary kept at this time records a pathetic failure to live up to the obligations of clerical celibacy. When he was a young man he had seen active service as a military chaplain in those days when the Swiss mercenaries, much sought after, were the best infantry in the world.

His sermons in Zurich comprised a commentary on the New Testament and, as time went on, various pulpit utterances showed the drift of his mind away from Catholic doctrine. He had always been antipapal, with a liking for the conciliar theory. In 1522 he broke openly with the Church—symbolically by a meat dinner with friends on Ash Wednesday—and somewhat later formally renounced his priesthood. By this time the Catholic cause was lost in Zurich. Zwingli was appointed official preacher by the town council. He was followed in his apostasy by other priests, many of whom found wives for themselves, some, like Luther's wife, nuns who had left their convents. The frequency of this sort of thing at the time gives cogency to a remark of the Swiss historian Burckhardt: "The Reformation is the faith of all those who would like not to have to do something any more."

At first Zwingli had been an admirer of Luther, although there were theological differences between them. Luther always retained a belief in the Real Presence in the Eucharist. Zwingli declared the Eucharist was a memorial only, the bread and wine remaining unchanged.

Before his early death on the battlefield in a civil war between Catholic and Protestant cantons (1531) Zwingli
met Luther. The encounter was not a success. Discussion
emphasized the differences in their ideas, and Dr. Luther
was never the man to hide his dislikes under a veneer of
politeness. Protestant Switzerland went her own way,
Zwinglian, not Lutheran, until Calvin came along and im-
posed his cast-iron system on the citizens of Geneva.

We cannot attribute directly to Luther the loss by the
Catholic Church of Holland, Scotland, a large part of
Switzerland, and a section of the French people. The full
development of some of Luther's ideas was not completed
until a generation after he had broken with the Church,
Then the work was done by a Frenchman, with clarity,
logic, and a cold, intellectual acceptance of consequences
which to us appear monstrous.

John Calvin (Jean Cauvin or Chauvin in French) was
born in 1509 at Noyon, in the north of France, where his
father was a church lawyer in the service of the bishop.
The father planned a church career for his son and so, in
accordance with the practice of the times, the boy was
tonsured and allotted a small income from a church living
when he was about twelve years old. Law, however,
seemed to offer better worldly prospects than the priesthood for the clever, studious schoolboy. He studied law
under several well-known professors in various places and
was much interested in the classical studies then popular.
He became a good Latinist and learned Greek. Some of
his time as a student was spent in the University of Paris,
where he was a member of the College of Montaigu. In
this college Erasmus had studied at one time and it was
here that St. Ignatius of Loyola finished his education and
collected his early followers, the future Jesuits.

We know little of the evolution of Calvin's religious
ideas during his formative years. Early in 1532 he was still
deep in law studies and the classics, but some time be-

tween April of that year and the winter of 1533 he underwent what he calls a sudden conversion, which he regarded as the direct result of God's action on his soul. Thereafter his progress towards the theological system we call Calvinism was rapid, logical and, granting its basic assumptions, consistent.

The young man fell under suspicion and was in prison for two short periods, but heretical teaching had not yet made much headway in France and the authorities were easygoing. Calvin was released, but when more serious danger threatened he fled to Switzerland for a time, studied Hebrew, and set to work writing his *Institutes of the Christian Religion,* in Latin, but later translated into French by himself. The doctrine of justification by faith is adopted from Luther, and then Calvin works out the concept of predestination—quite simply that God from all eternity chose to create certain human souls for eternal happiness, and others, the majority, for eternal misery in hell.

When, later, self-exile from France was the alternative to arrest and a probable execution for heresy, Calvin planned to go to Germany, but was persuaded to settle in Switzerland. Thus began his long domination, for some twenty-eight years until his death in 1564, of the civil and ecclesiastical authorities in Geneva. The paradox of his rule, as of traditional Calvinism everywhere, was the combination of belief in man's total depravity with the rigid imposition of the most exacting ethical code, both making up what we call Puritanism.

In 1553 occurred the event which forms posterity's gravest charge against Calvin. This was the execution— by fire—of the Spanish physician, anatomist, and amateur theologian Servetus (Miguel Serveto) on conviction of heresy. Servetus was anti-Trinitarian and denied the divinity of Christ, and was, therefore, obnoxious to both Catholics and Protestants. Calvin showed himself regrettably anxious for the imposition of the death penalty when Servetus had been convicted, and an obsolete law had to be revived for the purpose, the current maximum legal penalty being banishment.

Calvin's legacy to the western world was a harsh theological system and a rigid code of conduct. More immediately he was the source of the religious cleavage in France which gave that country a forty-year period of civil wars, marked by excesses of brutality, treachery, and fanaticism on both sides, including the horrors of the St. Bartholomew massacre.

6. Next to the destruction of the Catholic order in a large part of Germany, the greatest loss to the Church in the sixteenth century was that of England. It might even be argued that it was a greater loss. The culture of the English-speaking portion of the free world today is predominantly Protestant. But what if England, on the eve of her great overseas expansion, had remained in union with Rome? That, of course, is merely one of the ifs of history.

The loss of England was not *merely* the result of Henry's wanting a decree of nullity for his marriage with the Spanish princess of Aragon. Pope Clement VII (1523-1534) was, unfortunately, not the kind of cleric to deal successfully with the Tudor autocrat. He was virtuous, hard-working, well educated, but he was primarily a Medici nobleman rather than a dedicated spiritual leader. Worst of all, in dealing with an able, intelligent, strong-willed opponent like Henry Tudor he was irresolute and vacillating. His diplomacy was consistently unsuccessful. Throughout the seven-year struggle ending in the schism his policy was one of hoping for the best while the worst was taking place. Then we must take into account the ignorance and illiteracy of a large part, probably at least half, of the population. More distressing for English Catholics to contemplate is the supineness of what we call the intelligentsia, especially the clergy. There was a Catholic population of some four million, with which the heresies of the European continent had so far made only negligible headway.

Asked to name laymen heroic enough to stand up against the substitution of king for pope as ruler of conscience, we think of one—Sir Thomas More (canonized in 1935). In the ranks of the clergy we have one bishop, St. John Fisher of Rochester, a few monks (Carthusians), a few friars (Franciscans), and one Bridgettine priest. The last-named, however, was executed for his forcibly worded comments on the king's relations with Anne Boleyn. Five other priests who were put to death suffered as so-called accomplices, actually dupes, of a hysterical woman, Elizabeth Barton, who thought herself the subject of divine revelations. She had denounced Henry's marriage to Anne after Thomas Cranmer, the new archbishop of Canterbury, had assured the king of the invalidity of his marriage to Catherine of Aragon.

The story of the English break with Rome is a complex one and only a brief outline is possible in a short history of the Church. Henry and his ministers took between six and seven years (1527-1534) to break away entirely from Rome. The break was permanent, except for the five years of his daughter Mary's reign (Mary I, 1553-1558).

When Henry VIII began to hope for an annulment of his marriage, he was being well served by Cardinal Wolsey as his chief minister, a skilled administrator, enormously wealthy, proud, unspiritual until the last days of his fall from power. Wolsey worked hard to obtain what his king desired. He devised several plans, all of them frustrated by Catherine's strength of will and her determination not to yield either to bullying or cajolery. Then Wolsey received authority as papal legate for Clement

VII and was joined by Cardinal Campeggio, who had been the emperor Charles V's adviser in dealing with the Lutherans. The two legates were stalemated by Catherine's action in citing a papal brief which disposed of the arguments for the invalidity of her marriage to Henry. Campeggio shrewdly adjourned the proceedings.

Clement VII, after much indecision, transferred the case to his own courts in Rome. Wolsey had failed. His downfall followed and he died, disillusioned and repentant, in time to escape attainder and execution (1530). He was succeeded in office and in the king's favor by Thomas Cromwell.

Cromwell was a layman who had been Wolsey's factotum. Like his master he was of humble birth; he was also an adventurer and had been a *condottiere* (mercenary soldier) in Italy, merchant, money-lender, lawyer and, after Wolsey's fall, he was the most powerful man in England below the king. He was an enigmatic man. Although on his master's disgrace he stepped into the cardinal's position, he seems never to have spoken disloyally of Wolsey. His work to overthrow papal authority in England was probably a matter of politics and nothing else. To see him as an earnest Lutheran or a precursor of English Protestantism, as Foxe of *The Book of Martyrs* does, is wholly unhistorical. When he died, after miserably cringing to the tyrant king for mercy, he asserted that he died a Catholic. The only recorded instance of a display of any softer emotion by this sinister man is the evidence of a contemporary who once saw him in tears as he recited the *Little Office of the Blessed Virgin*.

In the years between his rise to power in 1530 and his execution in 1540 Cromwell wrought immense injury on the Catholic Church in England. He met his fate by overreaching himself in Machiavellian strategy. To bring Henry VIII closer to the German Protestant movement —a strange misjudgment of Henry's sympathies—Cromwell planned a royal marriage with the Lutheran princess, Anne of Cleves, and aroused the king's interest by accounts of the princess' charms and the display of a more than flattering portrait in oils. Anne's appearance when she reached England belied the reports and she was made the recipient of an early divorce and a generous pension. Cromwell paid for his miscalculation on the scaffold.

Towards the end of his life Pope Clement VII pronounced on the validity of Henry's marriage to Catherine of Aragon, but by this time England's unity with Rome had been destroyed. In 1533 Henry secretly married Anne Boleyn over the protests of the aged archbishop of Canterbury, William Warham, who died in time to escape the fate of those who opposed the royal will. The new archbishop, Thomas Cranmer, was a scholarly priest but one of a group of Lutheran sympathizers from the University of Cambridge. He was chosen by Henry but received the formal confirmation of the pope. Cranmer, of course, was made primate to do the king's bidding. He announced that the marriage with Catherine, widow of Henry's elder brother, Prince Arthur, had been invalid; he crowned Anne Boleyn as queen and stood godfather to her child, the future Queen Elizabeth I.

At this time took place the suppression of the monastic houses, first the smaller monasteries and convents on the score of laxity, the larger communities being spared as fervent and edifying. Somewhat later they, too, were suppressed; a valuable source of wealth was tapped by the deflection of their resources to the royal treasury after small pensions had been paid to the religious who could not be assimilated to the secular clergy.

Barefaced as most of the spoliation was—we read of cartloads of jewels, precious metals, and valuable fabrics carried off from such shrines as that of St. Thomas à Becket at Canterbury—this in itself did not establish a final break with Rome. Wolsey had, with papal approval, suppressed various small communities and used their money to endow an Oxford college and a grammar school in his native Ipswich. The culmination of Tudor absolutism in church matters came in 1534 with the Act of Supremacy, declaring the king to be the supreme head and governor on earth of the Church in England. The earlier qualifying clause, put forward by a timorous convocation of the clergy, "insofar as the law of Christ will allow," was left out by Parliament. An oath of acceptance of the royal supremacy was to be demanded of every English subject. Refusal was treason and carried the statutory penalty —beheading for the nobility and prelates, for the commoners hanging, that is, semi-strangulation followed by castration and disembowelling of the live victim. In both cases the convicted person's goods were confiscated.

Despite the repudiation of papal supremacy, the suppression of the religious houses, and the execution of the bishop of Rochester, John Fisher, and the ex-chancellor Sir Thomas More in 1535, the country was not yet in any true sense "Protestant." This is some explanation of what, viewed superficially, looks like nationwide apostasy. Externals were little changed, and a degree of learning and great strength of character were needed to perceive and withstand the innovation. The monastic houses had been closed or put to other uses, but the parish churches were untouched and priests still said Mass and administered the sacraments. Celibacy was still the law for the clergy, and the denial of certain Catholic doctrines and practices, including transubstantiation and confession, was punishable by death at the stake. Briefly, Henry VIII's church was "Anglican," with authentic priests and valid sacraments, not a Protestant institution. That came later, under the king's successor, Edward VI, the gifted but sickly boy born of Henry's third marriage. In the boy-king's reign the regents governing the country made over the new national church on Protestant lines, giving it a manual of worship, the Prayer Book, in Cranmer's magnificent English. This book was mostly on traditional Catholic lines as a work of devotion, but its theological definitions, "Articles" of religion, were Calvinistic.

When the precocious, tubercular king, aged sixteen, died in 1553, he was followed by his Catholic half-sister Mary, daughter of Henry's repudiated marriage with Catherine of Aragon. England was restored to Roman unity, but the queen's reign of five years was too short and her religious policy too ill-advised for the restoration to be permanent. Under her half-sister, Elizabeth I (1558-1603), the official religious pattern of the Anglican establishment was worked out, a *via media* or attempted compromise between Rome and Protestantism.

By the time the worried, hesitant Pope Clement VII died in 1534 the religious geography of what had been Christendom was a grim picture. Germany was torn in two and Lutheranism seemed to be making headway all the time. Switzerland was similarly divided into two warring factions and the Scandinavian countries were going over to the new doctrines. England was lost. In Scotland ecclesiastical life was at a low ebb and the country was ripe for upheaval and revolt. The Irish were attached to the Faith inherited from the missionary bishop St. Patrick, but their religious life and economic condition were both at the mercy of the English crown.

In France, heresy had gone underground but might emerge and win wide acceptance as it had done in the time of the Albigenses. Spain was deeply, even fanatically, loyal to Catholic tradition, and her missionaries were carrying the Faith to vast new areas across the Atlantic, but French rivalry and her own nationalism and the absolutist spirit of the Spanish monarchy often hindered rather than helped the action of the Papacy. Lastly, the unhappy memories of worldliness in the higher ranks of the hierarchy, of bishops or archbishops conferring benefices on their nephews or their own bastard children—all this lingered in men's minds and predisposed them to rebellion. Then there was the glaring maldistribution of wealth—the wretched serf or even the free laborer living on the verge of starvation much of the time and seeing his bishop, less often his parish priest, enjoying the amenities of the landowning class. There is no question that the immense holdings of land by church dignitaries or religious houses were a scandal to the laity, although it must be admitted also that clerical or monastic landlords were usually more humane than lay proprietors with families to enrich.

12. The Church and the Catholic Reformation (a)

1. A period of Catholic reform whose limits are, roughly, the middle of the sixteenth century and the end of the Thirty Years' War (1648), has come to be known as the Counter Reformation. The term, of non-Catholic origin, is now in general use, but this is to be regretted. It seems to imply, as it was at first meant to imply, that the Catholic movement was merely a belated response to the Protestant one which had swept over northern Europe since Luther nailed his theses to the door of the castle church of All Saints in Wittenberg in 1517.

This view is at variance with the facts. Whenever reform was needed within the Church, voices were raised to demand it. Sometimes they are the collective voices of many prelates, as in the fifth Lateran Council of 1512-1517; at other times an individual pontiff speaks his mind, as did the earnest Dutch pope, Adrian VI, at his election, lashing out against the sins of his predecessors and contemporaries. We shall see reforming popes, even sometimes when guilty of the things they denounce, condemning nepotism, or family favoritism, and pluralities, that is, the holding of two or more sources of church income at the same time.

The so-called Counter Reformation, then, did not follow the Protestant movement; it preceded it. Ecclesiastical historians see it foreshadowed in the Oratory of Divine Love, founded in Rome under Julius II (1503-1513), itself a revival of a similar fraternity connected with the late fifteenth-century mystic St. Catherine of Genoa. The members of this Roman association, priests and laymen, met regularly for spiritual devotions in one of the city's churches. Their specific object was personal sanctification, fruitful in Christian social service like that of the St. Vincent de Paul Societies in later times. The confraternity was already the training school of Catholic reformers before Martin Luther had evolved his theory of justification in the midst of his temptations, doubts, scruples, and all the mental agony of his Erfurt period.

The Roman Oratory of Divine Love gave the Catholic Church one of her great reformers of priestly life, St. Cajetan, founder with a fellow member of the Theatine order of clerks-regular, priests devoted to the work of parochial clergy but living under vow. Their vow of poverty was one of the strictest ever authorized; unlike the mendicant friars, they might not even beg; they could only take what was given them. The co-founder was the reforming pope, Paul IV. Other members became cardinals and were able to use the prestige of their rank as church reformers.

The assignment of dates for the Catholic Reformation is an arbitrary affair. Some historians take the pontificate of Paul IV (1555-1559) as their starting point. There is a good argument for tracing the movement further back, to Paul III (1534-1549), since it was he who convened the great reform council which set the pattern for the organized life of the Church as we know it. This is the nineteenth ecumenical council, that of Trent.* When Clement VII died in 1534, the cardinals chose a successor with remarkable speed and unanimity. Alessandro Farnese, an elderly administrator and scholar, of a noble family, was elected within a few hours of the conclave's assembling. Cardinal Farnese was no saint. His life as a cardinal not yet in priest's orders had not been blameless; it is said that as a young man he received the red hat because his sister, Giulia Orsini (Giulia Bella), was carrying on an adulterous liaison with Alexander VI. Farnese himself had several children in his younger days. He was always enough of the Renaissance grandee to see to their advancement even when he was working zealously for church reform. In middle life he turned over a new leaf, except for nepotism, received priest's orders, and when made a bishop showed himself an able and hard-working prelate. He was sixty-six when he became pope, but Titian's portraits of him as pope show the man he was, physically frail but with a piercing glance that hinted at the steely will under a diplomat's exterior.

At the time when the cardinals elected this Renaissance aristocrat as pope, one might have met in the streets of Rome a needy but happy-go-lucky young man, son of a not very prosperous lawyer in Florence. This young Filippo, whom Catholics venerate as St. Philip Neri, may be described as a saint in search of a vocation. He found it eventually in leading vast numbers of young Romans to sanctification and in reviving an almost forgotten trait in the life of the Roman clergy, sacerdotal zeal. It is interesting to contemplate these two reformers in their juxtaposition in time and place—the shabby young saint in the Roman streets and alleys and the wise old Farnese pon-

* There have been twenty such councils only. The last (the twentieth) was the Vatican Council of 1869-1870. The present pope has announced his intention to call the twenty-first Council.

tiff determined on thorough reform from the Vatican downwards.

2. Announcement of a forthcoming council was one of Paul III's early declarations as head of the Church. Unlike his predecessors, he was very much awake to the menace of Lutheranism. He saw, too, the double error that made the emperor, Charles V, an uncertain factor in a struggle for the integrity of the Church. Charles's Catholic loyalty was sound enough, but, like the emperors before him, he was sure that God meant the emperor to have the last word when pope and emperor differed. Furthermore, his second error was due to his concern about his restless Germanic provinces; he hoped a doctrinal compromise would pacify them. *Doctrinal* is the operative word; religious toleration as an accepted practice was still in the future.

Paul III convened his council but had much vexation and worry over it. He worked and struggled for it with characteristic tenacity, but he had been dead nearly fifteen years before it completed its task and was dissolved. The response to the first moves of the pope in the matter was discouraging. Neither France nor the emperor was cooperative. Then, when a site was to be chosen, there was more trouble. Paul wished it to be Mantua, but the duke of that city-state wanted armed forces to protect the council—at papal expense. In 1538 a start was made at Vicenza; the pope's three legates, the able cardinals del Monte and Cervini, both future popes, and Reginald Pole, the English cardinal of semiroyal blood, arrived at the meeting place. Finally, of the whole Catholic hierarchy, five bishops arrived. Of all the rest, some could not go because of local wars, others were forbidden by Council-shy rulers, and still others would not face the perils and hardships of foreign travel. Thus the matter stood until the winter of 1545. Meanwhile an event of profound significance for the Church's future took place.

An important problem of the Church lay before the pope and his reforming cardinals, Carafa, Contarini, and Morone, the last-named a man ahead of his era in holding firmly that heretics should be patiently reconverted rather than summarily executed. All were in agreement on the need for dealing with religious orders that had lost their fervor. So strongly did earnest churchmen feel about this that they were in favor of forbidding most of the orders to receive novices. The institutes would die out and at some time in the distant future a fresh start could be made. This is important in view of Paul III's action in 1540.

3. Several years earlier a small party of devout and well-educated young men of mixed nationalities had been presented to the pope. They offered him their services for whatever he could put them to. They were led by a Spanish ex-officer, of good parentage but less erudition than his followers and on the verge of middle age. This man, Iñigo of Loyola, a Spanish Basque by birth, who had adopted the patristic name Ignatius, had been lamed by a cannon ball at Pamplona on the Spanish border in a war between imperial Spain and France. A sickbed conversion, not in faith but in morals, voluntary poverty, experiences in mystical prayer and asceticism that produced *The Spiritual Exercises,* the drudgery of elementary-school studies, and then the gathering together of his little band of disciples—all at last brought him to the feet of the scholarly and shrewd pontiff in the papal palace. Ignatius' first ambition for his "company" (to him, *compañía* was a soldier's term, a commando force, we might say) had been Christian missionary work and a good chance of martyrdom among the Mohammedans of the Near East. The pope gave leave for ordination and for the journey to the Holy Land—if the party could get

there. Circumstances made the voyage impossible and now, in the spring of 1540, the young men were again in the pope's presence. Despite the warnings of his advisers, he had previously encouraged the volunteers to think of giving their association permanence as a religious institute.

They now had their plan down in black and white. It was a revolutionary kind of religious order—strict poverty, as well as chastity and obedience, like the traditional friars, but no fixed religious habit and, an unthinkable innovation in the eyes of conservative churchmen, no singing of the Divine Office in choir.

Even after his amendment of his ways in middle life and his ordination to the priesthood, Paul III remained a good deal the sixteenth-century nobleman in the See of Peter. He gave the cardinal's hat to both his grandsons, boys in their teens. Nevertheless the intuitions of a true ecclesiastic were in the eagle glance of the septuagenarian pope. He saw sanctity and ability in the limping, middle-aged Spaniard who knelt before him. *"Digitus Dei est hic"* ("The finger of God is here"), tradition reports him as saying when he had read the draft of Ignatius' scheme of religious life. On September 27, 1540, he issued the Bull *Regimini militantis ecclesiae,* and thus the Society of Jesus came into being. There were only ten members of the order, Jesuits, at first, and the Bull limited their number to sixty, but the restriction was done away with four years later. When Father-general Ignatius Loyola died in 1556 there were a thousand of them, scattered over the known world. There are now more than thirty-four thousand—all over the world. Indeed, it is difficult to picture the modern Church without the Jesuits.

4. The council for which Paul III had striven so long and so doggedly at length assembled as a going concern in the winter of 1545. The little town of Trent, ruled by a prince-bishop, was chosen for the meetings. Trent, in what is now an Italian province, was in imperial territory but near enough to Rome to prevent its domination by Charles V; the site was a working compromise between pope and emperor. Paul III lived until the end of the first active period of the Council, September 1549, and died less than two months later.

A conflict of wills between pope and emperor had threatened the success of the council at first. Paul III, aware of the chasm between Catholic and Lutheran theology, was insistent that the fathers of Trent should see to the definition of Catholic dogmas assailed by the new teaching. Charles V, torn between Catholic loyalty and political expediency, was fearful of driving his Lutheran subjects into open revolt and he wished the council to confine its efforts to the reform of abuses. The pope decided that both objectives must be kept in view. From the opening address to the assembled prelates by Cardinal Pole early in 1546 until its last session late in 1563 the council, of between fifty and sixty bishops accompanied by their attendant theologians and canonists, was faithful to Paul III's directive. Among the theologians who advised the bishops were members of the infant Society of Jesus. One of them was Diego Laynez, St. Ignatius' successor as general of the Jesuits. From time to time at Trent he engaged in verbal battle with a fellow Spaniard who also was a great theologian, the Dominican Melchior Cano.

While the council was busy with such fundamental topics as original sin, justification, the sacraments of baptism and confirmation, and the authority of the Scriptures, Charles V was having trouble with the Protestant princes who had banded themselves together in the League of Schmalkalden. He defeated them in a war they had begun. About this time, plague threatened the area around Trent and the assembled bishops voted to move down to

Italy. The emperor blamed the pope for this decision. The council, except for a few dissidents, moved to Bologna, where it was unable to achieve anything. Charles V, who had been attempting the impossible task of reconciling Catholics and Lutherans by the Interim of 1548, kept his imperial bishops in session at Trent. He appeared to be on the verge of schism and talked of an appeal to his rump council against the authority of the pope. Paul III showed patience and diplomacy, easing the tension by the dispersal of the assembly at Bologna; the bishops went home to their dioceses in the fall of 1549, and so the matter stood for a couple of years.

Paul III has been described as the last of the Renaissance popes; he was also the first of the reformers in the See of Peter in that era. His immediate successors inherited his zeal for reform but not his worldliness. The first two of them had both presided at the Council of Trent and both had to face the emperor's disfavor because of their loyalty to the Papacy. Paul III was followed by Cardinal del Monte as Julius III, whose pontificate of five years saw the reassembling of the council in 1551, the founding of the German College to train priests for work in the north, decrees against abuses in religious orders and against pluralities. The year before he died the pope sent Cardinal Pole to absolve England of schism and restore her to union with Rome under her Catholic queen, Mary I.

When Julius III died there was elected in his place another of the first Tridentine* legates, Cardinal Cervini. As Pope Marcellus II he might have speeded up the work of the Council of Trent, successfully opposed the imperial attempts at Catholic-Lutheran compromise, and achieved an early reform. Unhappily for the cause of reform he died less than three weeks after his election.

* *Tridentine* from the Latin name, *Tridentum,* of the city of Trent.

The accession in 1555 of Gian' Pietro Carafa as pope caused some uneasiness in Roman society. He had been archbishop of Naples, his native city; now, in his seventy-ninth year, he was regarded as, quite literally, a holy terror. He was deeply religious and ascetic in his own life and of draconian fierceness in dealing with every kind of wrongdoing. With the saturnine humor he sometimes allowed himself he said, on hearing he had received the majority vote in the conclave, that it must have been the Will of God, for never in his life had he done any man a favor.

The emperor had vetoed Carafa's election—in vain. The antipathy of pope and emperor was mutual. Paul IV, as he now was, distrusted the empire and loathed its Spanish subjects, nor did he ever conceal his sentiments with diplomatic courtesy in all his administrative experience—nunciatures in Spain and England, the archbishopric of Naples, the organization of the Roman Inquisition, and the censorship of books. He had given up all his dignities to assist St. Cajetan in founding the austere Theatine clerks-regular. Unfortunately Paul IV had an explosive temper, and his violent prejudices made enemies where the self-control of Ignatius Loyola or the good nature of Philip Neri would have won friends and allies.

The pope's distrust of councils, including his hostility to that of Trent, seems to have been part of his attitude to conferences in general and may have been strengthened by Charles V's compromise with the Protestant princes at the peace settlement of Augsburg (1555), a compromise that elevated into a principle the dictum *Cujus regio, ejus religio,* that is to say, the ruler's own religion, Catholic or Protestant, was the official one in his territory. His subjects had the choice of acceptance or leaving their country; the concept of objective truth was tacitly abandoned. The irascible old pontiff was a firm believer in direct action wherever the Holy See had the right to exercise it. For example, he ordered the Jesuits, whom he alternately caressed and nagged, to sing the Divine Office, like all monks and friars, despite the approval of their institute by Paul III. The Jesuits, of course, obeyed—with only moderate results—until the next pontificate. More serious was the pope's distrust of conciliar action. The meetings of the Council of Trent remained suspended.

Paul IV's hatred of the Spaniards affected his foreign policy, not unjustifiably, it would seem, in view of King Philip II's fondness for meddling with church affairs. The outcome was, however, disastrous. The pope made an alliance with the French, was outgeneraled and defeated by the redoubtable Duke of Alva and, after witnessing much loss and suffering, had to make the best terms he could with Spain. On his deathbed, in the torrid Roman summer of 1559, the old pontiff sent for Father Laynez, the Jesuit general, showed him money set aside for the endowment of the Roman College, expressed his love for the fathers of the Society whose peace of mind he had sometimes upset, and in touching words told of his own sorrow for mistakes of policy. "From the time of St. Peter," he said, "there has not been a pontificate more unhappy than the one now closing. I am truly sorry for all that has happened. Pray for me."

Not only in his dealings with Spain and France had Paul IV's policy been unfortunate. His attitude towards England's enigmatic new queen, Elizabeth I, probably tended to push her towards the final break with Rome. He wished to deal with Tudor England as a papal fief, as it had been for a time in the Middle Ages, and he seemed unaware that this was no longer practical politics. Philip II, who as the widower of Elizabeth's Catholic half-sister Mary I knew more about the situation, advised caution and an attempt to win the new queen to keep her promise to the dying Mary to maintain the Catholic Church in her realm.

The Catholic reform movement, which had started before Luther's revolt, gathered momentum under such energetic popes as Paul III and Paul IV and by the time of the latter's death had become a fixed tendency and a policy that would never be reversed. The reforms of Paul IV were continued by his successor Pius IV, a Medici of Milan, not of Florence, whose suavity and good nature achieved diplomatic successes by soothing the wounded feelings left by Paul IV's harshness.

Pius IV was well served by his cardinals. One of them was Giovanni Morone, who had worked for Paul III and Julius III on various diplomatic missions. Under Paul IV, incredibly, Morone was imprisoned along with Cardinal Pole, in the papal fortress of Sant' Angelo, on suspicion of heresy! The incident arose from the clash of temperaments, Paul IV's, harsh and despotic, that of Morone and Pole mild and opposed to persecution. Both cardinals wished to lead straying sheep back to the fold by reason and persuasion.

One of Pius IV's recipients of the cardinal's hat—at the age of twenty-two—was his nephew. Perhaps jealous voices muttered "Nepotism!", but the choice was a wise one. The young cardinal, still a student of theology, was ordained a priest and then consecrated archbishop of Milan three years later. He was St. Charles Borromeo, model of post-Reformation prelates, supporter of the Council of Trent and, like St. Philip Neri and the newly founded Jesuits, advocate of the almost forgotten practice of frequent communion.

In Trent the council held its final sessions in the old Romanesque cathedral from the early weeks of 1562 until the last meeting in December 1563. This last year was the most fruitful one. The number of bishops attending was nearly double that of earlier sessions. Politics and national rivalries were kept under stern control. Briefly we may say that at this time the assembled bishops rebuilt and strengthened a working organization which has served the Church ever since. Catholics of the twentieth century are Tridentine Catholics.

Two subjects received special attention towards the end of the council. The first one was clerical education. Every diocese was to have a seminary, with competent instructors, under the control of the bishop. Men destined for priestly work, either at home or on foreign missions, would henceforth be trained for their life, mentally as well as spiritually. No longer was there a place for the ignorant, semiliterate priest mumbling a liturgy he could barely read and utterly unfit to defend his teaching against learned opponents.

The other topic of importance in 1562-1563 was Christian marriage. The Council made a searching study of matrimony as both sacrament and contract and promulgated regulations to safeguard it against abuses.

13. The Church and the Catholic Reformation (b)

1. All lingering traces of the Renaissance Papacy disappeared with the election of Pius IV's successor. The choice of the Dominican Cardinal Ghislieri, a bishop and then Grand Inquisitor under Pius IV, was a victory for the reforming cardinals and for the influence of the cardinal archbishop of Milan, St. Charles Borromeo. The new pope, to be canonized in 1712 as St. Pius V, was a strict ascetic and a stern enemy to corruption. High rank no longer gave immunity from punishment for wrongdoing. One suspects that the pope was more pleased to order a public whipping for adultery in the case of an aristocrat than of a sinner in a humbler station.

As Pius V is one of the canonized saints of the Catholic Reformation his personal holiness is beyond question. Whether his political wisdom was always equal to his sanctity has been doubted. The doubt arises in regard to the Bull of 1570 by which he excommunicated Queen Elizabeth I of England, declared her a bastard and deposed her, and invited Christian princes to make the deposition a reality. The Bull *Regnans in excelsis* often left the persecuted English Catholics no choice between apostasy and martyrdom; it helped to sway the government of Queen Elizabeth towards the out-and-out Protestants, the Puritan wing of her national church whose mentality and mannerisms she herself loathed. The pope's deposing power had, at least in theory, been taken for granted in the Middle Ages. St. Pius V was not the only great churchman in his time who held that the power was divinely instituted. The great English Jesuit, Robert Persons, seems to have regarded this as a matter of faith binding on the conscience of Catholics.

Happier in its outcome was St. Pius's effort to unite Spain and the Venetian Republic in the Holy League to save the Mediterranean from becoming a Turkish lake. The naval victory of Lepanto (1571), in which the Turks were defeated by Charles V's bastard son, Don John of Austria, German by birth, Spanish by education, put an end to the menace of Moslem naval power.

The hope of restoring Catholicism in England and thereby strengthening the Church in Europe generally did not die with St. Pius V. Pope Gregory XIII, best known for the reform of the calendar under his aegis, favored the idea of Elizabeth's deposition but did nothing active about it. More important for Catholic recovery in northern lands and for the spread of Catholic belief beyond the seas was this pope's encouragement of Jesuit missionary zeal on two fronts, in northern Europe and in Japan.

Religious fervor born of the Catholic Reformation found an outlet in missionary activity at home as well as in the Far East or the new countries across the Atlantic. St. Philip Neri, an aging man and perhaps the best-loved priest in Rome, had transformed the spiritual life of the pope's Roman subjects. Matteo di Bascio's strictly reformed Franciscans, who were known as Capuchins, had, in less than fifty years, raised the level of Christian practice wherever the sandaled friars appeared among the poorer townsmen and villagers of Europe; they also worked with the colonists and the natives of North America. A revival of monastic life in Spain owed much of its vigor to the Carmelite reform of St. Teresa of Avila, who died while Gregory XIII was pope.

2. In his pontificate two Jesuits, the first of their order to do so, went to England to work among the persecuted Catholics alongside Cardinal Allen's secular priests* from Douai and Rheims. The mission of the two English Jesuit priests (1580), both Oxford men and converts from the newly established Anglican body, provides a story both thrilling and poignant of a Catholic "underground" similar to that of the early Church. About the head of Father Robert Persons, leader of the mission, controversy has raged because of his attitude to the pope's Bull against Elizabeth and because of this Jesuit's desire for the success of Philip II's Armada. No one, however, can withstand the charm of his friend's character, the martyr Blessed Edmund Campion, who died in London protesting his loyalty to his lady the queen—St. Pius V's Bull notwithstanding.

There has always been a bond of mutual respect and, with rare exceptions, genuine affection between the two great orders of friars, the Preachers (Dominicans) and the Friars-Minor (Franciscans). The friendship between the Dominican pope, St. Pius V, and a Franciscan friar from the Adriatic coast, Felice Peretti, may stand for a symbol of this bond. The pope befriended the zealous and learned friar, seventeen years his junior, who had risen from great poverty in his native Ancona. Pius made him a cardinal and, one may say, coached him to be his successor. It did not happen quickly. There was an inex-

* *Secular* priests live and work in the world bound by obedience to their bishops but not under the three vows taken by members of religious orders, who are known as *regulars,* because they live under a rule (*regula*).

plicable antipathy between Gregory XIII and the Franciscan cardinal, who lived in semiretirement all through Gregory's reign and busied himself with revising and editing the works of St. Ambrose. Cardinal Peretti was a man of sixty-four when he became pope in 1585.

The wave of reform did not slacken. The new pope, Sixtus V, was a prodigy of enterprise and energy. Nothing escaped his scrutiny, from the bettering of spiritual life to the city water supply for Rome. He gave special attention to the suppression of brigandage in his dominions. Gregory XIII had failed as a temporal administrator—in finance and in the policing of his kingdom. Sixtus, born in dire poverty and then in youth vowed to Franciscan austerity, was successful in overcoming his predecessor's bankruptcy and in putting down the brigands. The old fortress of Sant' Angelo was crammed with gold and silver by way of a reserve fund. As for banditry—the sight of decaying heads on poles in towns and villages deterred criminals and reassured peaceful citizens.

One of Pope Sixtus' most ardent wishes was for the recovery of England. For a long time he hoped to reconcile the queen, for whose personality he expressed a satirical respect. "What a woman!" he exclaimed, remarking that had she been a Catholic and he not a cleric they would have made a wonderful couple. Later, as it was clear that England was attempting a permanent halfway house between Catholicism and extreme Protestantism, the pope gave rather lukewarm approval to the invasion scheme of Philip II of Spain. He made a grant of money to the king but was skeptical of any chance of success; he seemed neither surprised nor perturbed when English seamanship and the autumnal storms—God's Hand, in Protestant eyes—brought about the defeat of the Armada. There was logic in the pope's attitude, not want of zeal. A victorious Philip II, Catholic though he was, might have meant danger to papal independence and ended with the pope's facing a situation like that between St. Gregory VII and the emperor Henry IV.

Philip II, despite reports, maybe exaggerated, of his sexual laxity, was sincerely Catholic, but he was a bureaucrat, a crowned civil servant with a passion for administrative detail. This included meddling with the organization of the Church. Sixtus V observed and opposed this trait, but when the pope died, circumstances played into the king's hands. There was a succession of three pontiffs, Urban VII, Gregory XIV, and Innocent IX, all unduly subservient to Spain and all elected in conclaves where Philip's supporters ensured a majority vote. Happily for the Church these popes had brief reigns, altogether about two years. The trend was reversed in 1592. A man as strong-minded as Sixtus V but combining more suavity with his piety and learning was elected. Cardinal Aldobrandini became Pope Clement VIII. He made friends with France, lifting the excommunication from her Huguenot Henry of Navarre (Henry IV) and welcoming him as a Catholic convert, how sincere we do not know. This was the occasion of Henry's alleged quip about Paris being worth a Mass. Anyhow the settlement brought peace to France, and for the Papacy a good insurance against Spanish domination.

Clement VIII has been accused of nepotism, but in his favor it is recorded that he took St. Philip Neri for his confessor and gave the cardinal's hat to the first great church historian of the modern world, another saintly Oratorian, Baronius. Clement likewise raised to the purple, despite their protests, two outstanding Jesuit theologians. These were the gentle, humorous St. Robert Bellarmine and the dour and difficult Spaniard, of putative Jewish descent, Toledo (or, Latinized, Toletus). The latter's intellectual ability much impressed the French philosopher Montaigne when he met him.

Roman hopes of England's return to Catholic unity

survived all that happened in the reign of Elizabeth I. When she died (1603) and the Scots king James VI became King James I of England, hopes ran high again. James had reacted against Presbyterianism and the long, nagging sermons he had been made to sit through and, moreover, he received assurances of Catholic loyalty in England. When he was safely on the English throne, Catholic hopes suffered a setback. His "Na, na, we'll nae need the Papists now" may be legendary, but it expresses his sentiment. The Gunpowder Plot, the scheme of a few desperate men, mostly Catholics, led to renewed persecution under the penal laws. It has been surmised, but not conclusively proved, that the plot was known to government agents in its early stages and helped on by them to make sure of convictions and the death sentence.

3.   In Germany the outlook was more encouraging. Where the breakaway from Rome had occurred, the tide had now turned. The Catholics of the western and southern states had for years been listless and apathetic, ready perhaps to succumb to the Lutheran influence if their rulers set the example. By Clement VIII's time all this had changed. The Catholic Church, with a growing body of educated clergy, was no longer on the defensive. So far as this was the work of one man, the credit goes to a Jesuit priest who died, aged seventy-six, at Freiburg im Breisgau in 1597.

Peter Canisius, who has been canonized and declared a Doctor of the Church, was a Hollander by birth and a subject of the empire. His fifty-four years as a Jesuit were mainly devoted to the reformation of Catholic life, especially among the clergy, in central and northern Europe. He had all the attributes needed for the work—intellect, eloquence, massive theological learning, skill as a writer. Learned discourses at Augsburg and the Council of Trent, many sermons, religious writings, including a popular catechism, as well as administrative work in the Society of Jesus, were the means he used. Much of his success was due to charm of personality; he won men's hearts before he touched their intellects. This trait and the aura of sanctity drew to him a youthful Polish nobleman studying at Dillingen, the Jesuit saint, Stanislaus Kostka, who died of fever in Rome while a novice at Sant'Andrea.

From Clement VIII's death in 1605 until the Thirty Years' War was ended by the Treaty of Westphalia in 1648 there is a period of church history spanning five pontificates in less than half a century, a strange era. Something of the fervor and energy of the Catholic Reformation has evaporated, but the impetus given by the Council of Trent and the reformist popes carries the movement forward. Nepotism, display and extravagance, political bargaining with secular rulers—these things reappear from time to time. Nevertheless, the four pontiffs concerned— for Leo XI survived his election so short a time that we may omit him—were good churchmen and in one way or another gave something of value to the life of the Church.

Paul V, a Borghese, conscious of his own noble birth and of the rights of the Holy See, fought Gallicanism, the disruptive nationalistic spirit in the French Church. He canonized Milan's saintly archbishop, St. Charles Borromeo, and he was a good friend to the missionaries and the religious orders. He did much for the papal city, not omitting his own family monument, the Borghese Palace, started in his reign. His successor, Gregory XV, canonized four of the great saints of the Catholic Reformation, the two Jesuits St. Ignatius Loyola and St. Francis Xavier, Philip Neri, and the Carmelite reformer, Teresa of Avila. Gregory, too, was a friend to the foreign missions, and to him the Church owes the Congregation *De Propaganda Fide,* the papal headquarters for all missionary enterprise.

Urban VIII, of the powerful Florentine family of the Barberinis, was another zealous pontiff, yet not without a worldly streak; like Gregory XV, he left a monument to his family pride, the Barberini Palace. Withal he was a friend to missionary work and he was a guardian of religious orthodoxy, as shown in his condemnation of Jansenism. In conjunction with the rulers of Venice he sought to mediate in the Thirty Years' War and bring to an end the senseless killing and devastation, but France had entered the conflict along with her Swedish allies and was unwilling to talk of peace. As a highly civilized man and a priest, Urban was appalled by the havoc wrought by this war, but he concluded that it had become a purely political struggle and he shifted papal support from the empire to the French. An irony of this was that the Papacy became the friend of France's Swedish, and fanatically Protestant, allies.

Innocent X (1644-1655) outlived the Thirty Years' War and protested against the cynical disregard for the rights of the Church and of private conscience in the peace treaties of 1648. The character of reformer comes out in this pope; he was earnest in support of monastic ideals and their restoration when practice had grown lax. In the Jansenist controversy in France he intervened strenuously on behalf of Roman authority.

The Thirty Years' War was actually a series of wars and is strictly a matter of secular rather than religious history, as Urban VIII and Innocent X perceived. Although it started as a religious conflict between the Lutheran princes and the emperor, it lost all semblance of religious motive when France, under the guidance of her intensely nationalistic Cardinal Richelieu, entered it with Lutheran allies. Protestant fought Protestant and Catholic slaughtered Catholic with equal ferocity.

The Treaty of Westphalia, actually two treaties, one between the emperor and the French, at Münster, the other between the Swedes and the emperor, at Osnabrück, forms the last scene in the destruction of medieval Christendom. It revived the idea of royal absolutism in religious matters by which at Augsburg in 1555 the emperor had tried to reconcile the claims of Lutherans and Catholics. This was the major offense in Catholic eyes. There was incidental injustice in countenancing royal and princely seizures of church property. Innocent X protested, but his protests were disregarded. Henceforth the concept of the Church as a divinely founded arbiter in international affairs was, for all practical purposes, dropped by secular rulers. The Catholic Church would be, to them, only *a* church and very soon would be tolerated, if at all, only as a sect in many countries.

The period between the beginning of the Protestant Reformation and the time of the Thirty Years' War deserves our attention for its evidences of the spiritual life of Catholicism beneath all the national or racial impulses and the turmoil of quarrels between Church and State. This spiritual life, one of whose fruits is apostolic zeal, gave birth to great missionary undertakings in the period of transition that divides the Middle Ages from the post-Reformation era.

4. The new-found world of the Americas has its own record of sanctity and missionary fervor. Against the rapacity and cruelty of the Spanish conquistadors we must set the humanity of the Spanish missionary bishop Bartolomeo de las Casas, a Dominican, the "Apostle of the Indies." In central America and the Caribbean he was both Christian missionary and ardent fighter against the enslavement and exploitation of the native races. His scheme for an Indian commonwealth was eventually made a reality by the Jesuits in the Paraguay Reductions, an achievement in cooperative Christian living that has not yet been duplicated. In what is now Colombia, St. Peter Claver passed his Jesuit years as the "Apostle of the Negroes." It was a lifetime given to the most abject and wretched of all victims of man's inhumanity to man, the imported African slaves.

The way of the missionaries in North America, Franciscans, Jesuits, Sulpicians, was one of suffering, hardship, and incessant labor, often ending in martyrdom. The story of the North American martyrs in what is now eastern Canada and the northern part of New York State is one of almost unbelievable cruelties perpetrated on the French Jesuit fathers whose spiritual offspring afterwards put forth their own exemplars of sanctity.

The Jesuit Society had launched missionary enterprises in the Far East as soon as the pope had given his approval to the new order. St. Francis Xavier reestablished in India the Catholic Christianity taken there originally in the very early age of the Church, traditionally in the lifetime of the Apostles. Then he set up Catholic centers in Japan, destined to be nurseries of confessors and martyrs in the bitter persecutions which came after the saint's death.

In India the work of Christian evangelism was carried into the supposedly inaccessible Brahmin class by the so-called "Christian Brahmin," the Italian Jesuit, Robert de' Nobili. Another Italian Jesuit, Matteo Ricci, similarly broke through the exclusiveness of Chinese Mandarin society and won imperial favor and support. Unhappily, the prospect thus opened up of a large-scale Christian movement in China was destroyed by the jealousy of rivals of the Jesuits and by the maladroit action of a church official sent to the Far East to investigate the affair.

Two institutions for providing recruits for the expanding work of overseas missionary work arose in the later years of the Catholic Reformation. The Barberini pope, Urban VIII, in 1627 established a college for training missionaries, the College of Propaganda as it is called, one of the most important of all papal enterprises in clerical education. A foundation (1665) with kindred aims, but in this case part of the revival of priestly life in post-Reformation France, was the *Missions Étrangères* (Foreign Missionary College) in Paris. From its earliest days this college has prepared its dedicated young men for overseas work, its training a conscious and detailed forming of mind and heart for a life of toil, hardship, renunciation and, often, violent death.

5.   The goal of all church organization and activity is, of course, personal holiness, an axiom that became more and more widely appreciated in the age of reformation. We see it in the widespread adoption by the laity of religious practices once looked upon as something only for priests, monks, and nuns—daily meditation and examination of conscience, spiritual reading, periodical religious retreats. The lasting popularity of a religious book of the period, the *Introduction to the Devout Life,* is significant. Its author, the saintly and attractive bishop of Geneva and co-founder of the Visitation Order, St. Francis de Sales, wrote in French, not in Latin. His book he intended primarily for the laity. There had been spreading over the Catholic world at this time a devotion now universal in the Church, that of the Sacred Heart. It had its origins in the mystical life of a French Visitation nun, St. Margaret Mary Alacocque, directed by a Jesuit priest, Blessed Claude de la Colombière. He first preached the new form of devotion to Christ as Incarnate Savior in heretical England under the penal laws, when he was a chaplain at the court of Charles II's brother, the Duke of York, who was afterwards the ill-starred King James II.

The movement to foster priestly ideals in community life which St. Philip Neri had started in Rome with his Oratorians had its counterpart in France when Cardinal de Bérulle founded his own Oratory. Jean Jacques Olier had the same work in mind, strictly for the French secular clergy, when he founded in Paris the great seminary of Saint Sulpice.

Standing out above all his contemporaries is St. Vincent de Paul. In the course of his long life, eighty-five years, he founded a congregation of priests, the Lazarists or Vincentians, whose influence was first brought to bear on the life of rural France. Since then it has extended its field of work to include missionary, parochial, and educational labors in many countries of the world. St. Vincent is above all things the great Christian philanthropist, whose Sisters of Charity set the pattern for a new religious life for women, inwardly one of monastic renunciation, outwardly one of uncloistered social service.

Spain, scarcely touched by the new Lutheran and Calvinist theologies, showed the influence of the reform movement especially in monastic life. There took place what is probably the best known of all such reforms, that of the Carmelites by St. Teresa and her friend and disciple, the poet and mystic St. John of the Cross. The Spanish Franciscans had their own reformer and mystic, St. Peter of Alcantara.

Of the great amount of theological learning the Catholic Reformation era handed on to posterity, much still remains standard material in Catholic higher studies. There are the voluminous works on philosophy by the Jesuit St. Robert Bellarmine and the writings of his fellow Jesuits Suarez and Vasquez. Still respected by historical scholars are the *Ecclesiastical Annals* of St. Philip Neri's friend and successor in the government of the Roman Oratory, Cesare Cardinal Baronius, one of the most fair-minded of church historians.

14. The Church in the Age of Absolutism

1. Two tendencies appeared in the late Middle Ages, grew rapidly, and were widespread during and after the Lutheran movement. We call them royal absolutism and nationalism; the first has disappeared from our western world, but the second is still with us. Both are moods or climates of opinion opposed to the Catholic spirit.

In the period, slightly less than a century and a half, between the Treaty of Westphalia (1648) and the outbreak of the French Revolution (1789) the Catholic Church was at war with royal absolutism and nationalism. She suffered in these struggles, but in the later tranquil interval she emerged the stronger for the trials endured. Contemporary with the assault from absolutism and nationalism were certain new heresies which added to her troubles.

During this period France was the scene of the severest trials the Church had to face. Lutheranism gained no foothold in France, but the teaching of John Calvin, a Frenchman in exile, was held tenaciously by those of his countrymen known as Huguenots. For some thirty years of the sixteenth century French Catholics and Prot-

estants were engaged in the so-called religious wars—
"so-called" because they became, like the Thirty Years'
War, brutal contests for power. In 1572 the queen-regent,
Catherine de'Medici, precariously in power, ordered the
massacre of Protestants on St. Bartholomew's Eve, alleg-
ing in justification an imaginary plot against her son's
throne. This explains the seemingly deplorable rejoicing
in Rome when the news was carried there. When the last
Valois king, Henry III, was assassinated, the crown passed
to the Protestant king of Navarre. In 1593 he was reconciled to the Church; this may or may not have been mere
political expediency, but it brought the senseless fighting
to an end. Thereafter, with intervals of reactionary legislation, France would follow a policy of religious toleration, but Protestantism would not again seriously disturb
the Catholic Church in France. Her troubles would arise
among her own children.

From very early Christian times, thinkers had brooded
on the problem of reconciling belief in divine grace and
in God's foreknowledge with the freedom of man's will.
Patristic theologians, notably St. Augustine, had handled
the subject cautiously, but their caution left room for
other thinkers to take extreme positions. Thus it had happened with one of the heretics attacked by St. Augustine,
Pelagius, the British monk who exalted free will as the
sole necessary agent of salvation. The discussion continued
in the Church; orthodox theologians, bound to accept
both grace and freedom of the will, devised *theories* as to
the relation between the two. The opposing theories became associated with two religious orders, the Preachers
or Dominicans and the Jesuits. The controversy, which
sometimes led to an exchange of invective, was finally put
an end to by papal orders early in the seventeenth century. Obedient friars and Jesuits obeyed the injunction.

2. The obedience of these religious men was not the

end of the matter. John Calvin's doctrines of human depravity and of God's arbitrary predestination of human souls had long since been condemned, but his teaching reappeared in a modified form among French Catholics. This we call Jansenism, after a Dutch Catholic professor of theology, Cornelis Jansen, who became a bishop in Flanders. Bishop Jansen was an earnest cleric unaware that his theology was unsound. His book *Augustinus* was not published until after his death. He shared his ideas, many of them derived from an earlier writer, Baius, with a French friend, Jean Duvergier de Hauranne, the Abbé de Saint Cyran.* Saint Cyran and his friends the Arnaulds worked up the ideas of the Dutch professor into a puritanical and predestinarian system that has been described as Catholic Calvinism. It insisted on the small number of the saved, discouraged frequent communion, and branded as unworthy states of life, wherein salvation was virtually impossible, marriage and the world of commerce. The whole thing formed a body of gloomy belief and practice, but it seduced many devout minds by its austerity. Jansenist influence lingered in France and, perhaps, has not wholly died away. The powerful minister of state, Cardinal Richelieu, who was its enemy, imprisoned Saint Cyran for a time. The Jesuits fought the teaching with books, pamphlets, sermons, and spiritual direction, which drew upon them the enmity of Jansenism's most gifted convert, Blaise Pascal, mathematical genius, religious philosopher, master of French prose, but a neurotic. His *Provincial Letters,* against the Jesuits, were brilliant, witty, amusing and, as propaganda, unscrupulous. They did the French Jesuits much harm.

Jansenism, defying papal authority and seeking to narrow the field of papal infallibility, had a kinship with

* *Abbé* not in the modern French sense of an assistant priest or curate, but *abbot*—of an abbey held *in commendam,* that is, with the holder of the title drawing the revenue but having no administrative duty.

another aberration of Catholic orthodoxy in France, Gallicanism. Often this was more a state of mind than a definite doctrine. It can be traced back to the Middle Ages and it made a fresh appearance when Jansenist teachings were condemned by three successive popes in the middle years of the seventeenth century. A schism that would have involved a small party of French bishops was averted by the diplomacy of Pope Clement IX. Jansenism as a body of definite doctrine faded into the background of French religious thought, but the Gallicanism that had come to life during the controversy caused trouble when Louis XIV was king.

3. Louis's *L'état, c'est moi* ("*I* am the State"), if he indeed uttered the words, is bad enough; far worse was his virtual extension of the sentiment to the Church in France. An earlier French king, Francis I, also a monarch with absolutist ideas, had made a concordat (agreement) in 1516, receiving the right to the income of certain French sees when they were vacant. There were other privileges, allowed either by custom or explicit concession to the kings of France, and these made up the so-called "Liberties of the Gallican Church." The kings were very jealous about these *Regalia,* often pushing their claims to the verge of schism.

Louis XIV, looking about for much-needed funds, sought to relieve the strain on his exchequer by bringing all French sees under the terms of the concordat. The pope, Innocent XI, condemned this exercise of royal absolutism, whereupon an assembly of the French clergy in 1682 issued their *Four Articles,* an official declaration in favor of the superior authority of council over pope and adding what was practically an assertion of belief in the divine right of kings. Louis's clergy were then ordered by the king to impose acceptance of the *Articles* on professors in seminaries and all graduates in theology.

The pope, of course, vetoed the declaration and refused to grant bishoprics to clerics who had a hand in the affair. Louis, who had the right to nominate candidates for sees, refused to choose any except from the assembly. This stalemate lasted for ten years. By the end of the time about three dozen French sees were without bishops. The peace was made by another pope, Innocent XII. The royal command to impose the *Articles* on the seminaries was withdrawn and the pope agreed to accept Louis's nominees for the vacant bishoprics. Gallicanism, as a state of mind, did not entirely die out. The Dominicans and the Jesuits, who had often fought over theories of grace and free will, were united in their loyalty to Rome in these years.

4. Jansenism was by now merely a mood, sullen, wary, dour, inclined to treat the Papacy with silence and attack it by indirection—in the form of hostility to its champions, the Jesuits. The ending of the *Regalia* dispute was an uneasy compromise between Louis XIV's sense of divine right and the acceptance of papal supremacy in religious matters. Anyhow, the French Church might now, it was hoped, be left in peace to attend to the spiritual life of her members. From a genuine concern for spirituality, however, arose a new heresy, Quietism. Some authorities have thought the word "heresy" too strong a term for it. We may admit that in a modified form, as an attitude to spiritual reality, it is found in certain oriental religions and something akin to it enters into Christian mysticism.

The Quietism which disturbed the Catholic Church at the end of the seventeenth century arose in Spain. Its apostle was a priest, Miguel de Molinos, whose book, *Guida Spirituale,* caused him to be examined by the Roman Inquisition after he had settled in the papal city. The most suspect feature of his teaching was the insistence on a passivity of the human will in the presence of God so absolute that "good works" seemed to become unimportant. The "higher" nature of man was thus *separated,* not merely *distinguished,* from the "lower." A dangerous kind of moral indifference might then follow from this concept. Molinos was thrown into prison where, ten years later, he died. Evidently he had satisfied the authorities about his state of mind, for he was allowed to receive the last sacraments.

Meanwhile his mystical theology had gained widespread acceptance among the devout in France, where it had a devoted propagandist in a remarkable woman, Madame Guyon. She was a widow in early middle age at the time when Molinos was in trouble in Rome. Wealthy and pious, she had, we are told, much personal charm. In Paris she became friendly with the future archbishop of Cambrai, Fénelon, who was impressed by her ideas and embodied them in a devotional book, *Maxims of the Saints.* Later, this book was condemned by Rome; Fénelon, who had some of the qualities of sanctity, promptly submitted and made a retraction. Madame Guyon was imprisoned for a time, released, and sent to Meaux to be under the eye of Bishop Bossuet, who had for a time been sympathetic to Molinos's teaching but had come to hold it erroneous. Madame Guyon fled from Meaux without the bishop's consent, but she was finally allowed to settle down in peace on a country estate, where she lived the life of a *dévote* until her death in 1717. By that time Quietism no longer troubled the French Church. Jansenism had come to the front again.

5. The Jansenists engaged in a bitter controversy about the condemnation of Jansen's teaching. The propositions condemned were, they admitted, heretical, but they denied they were in the book *Augustinus* at all; the pope, moreover, although infallible in doctrine, was not so on

questions of fact. The Jansenists proposed an attitude of respectful silence—actually a kind of passive resistance. This, said Rome, would not do. The Jansenists had the support of Cardinal de Noailles, archbishop of Paris, but in 1713 the Bull *Unigenitus* condemned Jansenistic teaching so comprehensively that we may regard it as giving the death blow to the system within the Church. The cardinal had been excommunicated, but made his peace with Rome before his death some years later. The Jansenists blamed the issue of the Bull, as well as its severity, on the Jesuits.

The Jansenist opposition to the Society of Jesus led to a strange alignment of forces, for these Catholic puritans now found themselves, as enemies of the Jesuits and as critics of the Papacy, allies of the *philosophes* in Paris, that is, the group made up of Deists, skeptics, and avowed atheists, all hostile to organized Christianity, who would soon find their leader in a brilliant young man, a former pupil of the Jesuits, who had recently been imprisoned, mildly, for alleged disrespect to the regent. François Marie Arouet, whom we generally speak of as Voltaire, was not yet famous.

Events were now moving towards one of the worst calamities to befall the Church in the eighteenth century, the collaboration of Jansenists, Deists, freethinkers and Gallican members of the Paris *Parlement,* a royal mistress, and Bourbon rulers to destroy the Society of Jesus. Of these various groups the Jansenists alone were much interested in theology. Their rigorism found Jesuit moderation, which they called laxity, obnoxious. The Gallicans disliked Jesuit devotion to the Papacy. The Deists owed their philosophy largely to the English thinker John Locke. They believed in natural religion, the logical acceptance of a Supreme Being, Aristotle's First Cause, known by deductive reasoning. Revelation and belief in the supernatural they rejected. Authority in religious matters was abhorrent to them, hence their dislike of the Church, Voltaire's *infâme* ("the infamous thing").

The Bourbon rulers of France, Spain, Portugal, Naples, and the duchies of Parma and Lucca were Catholics, but all were absolutists, obsessed by the concept of the divine right of kings and, as pendant to it, of an extreme form of nationalism. The Jesuits, by the very nature of their order, were opposed to this, but we should distinguish between their Catholic attitude and the internationalism which decries all patriotism. Jesuit opposition to royal absolutism is implied by the typical Jesuit philosophy of government, surprisingly modern in spirit, which may be found in the writings of St. Robert Bellarmine. He was a pupil of Mariana, a Spanish Jesuit whose views on tyrants went to lengths that caused him to be silenced by the father-general of the order.

The campaign of the *philosophes,* which included the great mathematician d'Alembert and the gifted, hard-working editor of the *Encyclopédie,* Denis Diderot, was merely a war of words; actual power was in the hands of the Bourbon rulers, who regarded themselves as loyal to the Church.

The first open assault on the Jesuit Society took place in Portugal. The Bourbon king, Joseph I, was a nonentity without initiative except in the pursuit of his subjects' wives; the government was in the hands of his able, ambitious and unscrupulous minister, José de Carvalho, the Marquis of Pombal. Pombal had once been ambassador to England and had come back a Deist and a hater of papal authority. More understandable as a motive for his attitude to the Jesuits was his fear of their influence on his political future. Were they to bring the dissolute Joseph to a sense of duty, the Marquis's power would be in danger. So would his income, derived from monopolies. He started with a complaint to Rome, charging the Jesuits with dabbling in commerce, because they sold farm produce for the benefit of their Indian villages in the Paraguay Reductions.

The cardinal-archbishop of Lisbon, known to be unfriendly to the Jesuits, was told to make an enquiry. Within two weeks he had found them guilty—without their being heard in their own defense. Pope Benedict XIV died before he could look into the matter. His successor, Clement XIII, was known as a good friend to the Jesuits.

A sordid incident gave Pombal the opportunity he needed. One night a husband wronged by the king took a shot at the unworthy monarch, but missed. Pombal at once had recourse to a time-worn device—"A Jesuit plot!" "Jesuit tyrannicide!" There was no plot, but Pombal had the Jesuits arrested in their residences, schools, and churches. Some were thrown into dungeons to live or die; the rest were crowded on to ships, taking nothing but their breviaries or rosaries and the clothes they wore, and were dumped on the shores of the pope's dominions. All the property of the Portuguese Province of the Society of Jesus was confiscated (1759).

6. What happened in France provides equally depressing reading. Louis XV was another Bourbon with a streak of lechery. He had pious intervals when, brooding on hell fire, he would frequent the sacraments, abandon his lights o' love, and be faithful to his long-suffering Polish wife. Unfortunately for the Jesuits, the mistress who dominated him was a woman of charm, intelligence, strength of will and, for her own reasons, hostility to the Jesuits. The Marquise de Pompadour, Madame D'Étioles by marriage, had at first been friendly to the Jesuit fathers, from whom she chose her confessor. When, however, they would not tacitly condone royal adultery, her friendliness changed to enmity. The Abbé de Bernis, later a cardinal, who was no friend to the Jesuits, laid on the Pompadour the whole

responsibility for the ill-treatment of them and even for the suppression of the order.

Cardinal de Bernis exaggerated the Marquise's part in what was done. The effective agent of it was Étienne François, Duc de Choiseul. He was an able man, successful in war and diplomacy, worldly, but not unamiable. We do not know that he had any special prejudice against the Jesuits, but he was an opportunist who owed his political position to the Pompadour. The tide was running against the Jesuits; Choiseul always swam with the tide.

Choiseul was more honest, or more lucky, than Pombal. He did not invent an "incident" to give himself a handle against the Jesuits. A member of the Society unwittingly put it directly into his hands. Father La Valette, in charge of a mission station on the French West Indian island of Martinique, had gone beyond his authority in commercial dealings which had started innocently with the sale of produce for his Indian parishioners. He speculated on unharvested crops, bought stocks of produce outside his own mission—and met with bad luck. British naval vessels, as an act of war, seized his cargoes. He found himself in debt to a Marseilles brokerage firm for a sizable fortune, about two million French livres (in terms of relative purchasing power, several million dollars). The creditors, themselves in trouble, sought payment from the French Jesuit Province. The fathers in Paris denied responsibility, because the foreign missions were independent financially and Father La Valette had exceeded his powers. Perhaps the Jesuits would have been better advised to pay up and accept the loss. They acted without any of the cunning they are often credited with. They appealed to the *Parlement,* full of their enemies, and there was a long-drawn legal battle, but the outcome was inevitable. An edict expelling the Jesuits from France was placed before the king and after a struggle he signed it in 1764. Pope Clement XIII had the moral courage which Louis XV lacked. The papal Bull *Apostolicum pascendi munus* of the following year was a vindication of the Society.

7.   In Spain the attack on the Jesuits was similar to that in Portugal. The king took his cue from a powerful minister, and there was a public "incident," a ridiculous agitation over a piece of minor legislation. The only thing the Jesuits had to do with it was the quelling of a riot. That did not save them from charges of guilt and they were condemned without evidence in their defense. The Spanish king's motivation is less clear than that of the king of Portugal. Charles III of Spain was not a debauchee like Joseph of Portugal nor a man of Louis XV's weak character. Charles was a strict Catholic of a narrow-minded type. His minister, the Count of Aranda, a haughty aristocrat, was less venal than Pombal and less a careerist than Choiseul. He was a Voltairean Deist, possibly a skeptic, and perhaps he truly thought the presence of the Jesuits an obstacle to "progress," that pathetic illusion of the eighteenth-century followers of the "Enlightenment." In 1767 the expulsion of the Jesuits from all Spanish territory took place. The edict signed by the king stated no reasons; they were, it said, locked within the royal bosom. The harm wrought on the Church in Spain was dwarfed by the mischief overseas. The total fabric of the Paraguay Reductions was destroyed and with it the happiness, security, and future welfare of a whole Indian population. All the Jesuits in the Spanish colonial lands were at once put on ships and sent to the Papal States. The conditions of the fathers and brothers expelled from South America were even worse than those of their brethren in Spain. The Christian apostolate of the Jesuits in India and China was similarly brought to a stop by the colonial powers of Spain and Portugal.

8. The lesser Bourbons of Naples and Parma followed the example of the more powerful members of the clan and the whole group was now ready for an all-out attack on the Jesuit order. When it was made, circumstances favored the attackers. The new head of the Jesuits, Lorenzo Ricci, was a holy man, but no fighter. Clement XIII had died in 1769 and been succeeded by the Franciscan cardinal, Ganganelli, as Clement XIV. He, too, was a good man, but not of the caliber of St. Gregory VII or Innocent III. The Bourbons, through their ambassadors, worked on him by bullying, cajolery, pretence of reforming zeal and, worst of all, the threat of schism. The unhappy pope, as St. Alphonsus Liguori called him, finally gave way, sacrificing a mast to save the ship, in his own metaphor. He issued the Brief *Dominus ac Redemptor noster,* suppressing the Society of Jesus, in the summer of 1773. The pope, like Charles of Spain, kept the reasons for his act a secret in his heart. Thus was completed what Pius XI called "a painful page of history."

The document of suppression was a brief, not a bull. A bull is, simply by being issued, mandatory; a brief is operative only when promulgated. Here, then, is an ironical incident in the story of the Catholic Church. The "Most Christian King" (of France), the "Most Catholic King" (of Spain), and the Catholic rulers of Portugal, Naples, and Parma had treated the Jesuits as criminals and joined forces with the Deists and freethinkers to achieve the suppression of the Society. Two monarchs refused to allow the brief to be promulgated in their dominions. They were the Voltairean Frederick II ("the Great") of Prussia and the nominal Lutheran turned Russian Orthodox for reasons of state, the empress Catherine of Russia. A truncated but authentic Jesuit body went on with its work, chiefly educational, in Prussia and in White Russia. The latter territory was Catherine's share in the Partition of Poland.

9. Eighteenth-century absolutism allied itself with nationalism and, when professedly Catholic, tended to support the theory of council superiority to the decisions of popes. The Habsburg empress of Austria, who had shared in the spoliation of Poland, was encouraged in absolutist tendencies by her very able statesman Wenzel von Kaunitz. Her son, the emperor Joseph II, "my cousin the sacristan," as Frederick the Great contemptuously called him, was guilty of intolerable royal interference with the Church. In fact, devout Catholic as he claimed to be, he seems to have regarded the Church as a department of his civil service. Nothing in ecclesiastical affairs was left untouched; he meddled in the reform of religious orders, the management of seminaries, the liturgy, even details of church vestments and altar candles. At one period an Austrian schism threatened Catholic unity, and Pope Pius VI went in person to Vienna to avert the worst outcome of Joseph's actions. He was received with great ceremony but was able to accomplish only part of what he had hoped. This was in 1782, less than a decade before the French Revolution threatened both Papacy and kingship.

The movement for state supremacy over the Catholic Church received support in the German territories of the empire from a bishop, Nicholas von Hontheim. Writing under the pen name of Febronius, whence the name Febronianism for his teaching, he tried to revive the old imperial claims to dominate the Papacy. He said little that was original, but had a certain following among his brother bishops and so was the cause of some unrest. His book was condemned by Rome, he made a retraction in 1778 and died peacefully a dozen years later, but he had supplied material for more thoroughgoing revolutionaries who were to come after him.

The election of Pius VI in 1775 was regarded hopefully by the Bourbons, who looked to him to continue the policy of Clement XIV in regard to the Jesuits. Others, who perhaps knew more of the true mind of the successor to the Franciscan pope, thought he cherished a secret sympathy for the dispossessed Jesuits. It is certain that as the French Revolution ran its course and an actress was installed in Notre Dame as goddess of reason where Frenchmen had heard Mass in a cathedral dedicated to Mary, many others besides the pope saw good reason to mourn the disbanding of the Society of Jesus, a stabilizing influence in a world that was restless and about to overthrow institutions that had, it thought, become obsolete.

10. A superficial glance at eighteenth-century Catholicism inclines one to think that the Catholic Church had lost some of the spiritual energy and drive of preceding eras. Had she, one asks, fallen gently into a state of lethargy in which faith would slowly decay and such things as heroic sanctity and Christian mysticism would be only memories of an age and a kind of life no longer on the earth? For tokens of the inner vitality of the Catholic Church in any period of her history we turn to the records of achievement in the highest of all forms of human activity, that of holiness.

For such tokens of her enduring life in the eighteenth century we may well select two of the saints for whose holiness the Church has vouched officially by canonization. Two years after the Jesuits had been suppressed and royal absolutism seemed to have won a great triumph there died in Rome an Italian priest, by birth Paolo Francesco Danei, in the Church's calendar St. Paul of the Cross, founder of the Passionists. This religious congregation has always been known for its austerity of life and its zeal in preaching—like the first St. Paul—Christ crucified. The founder was the antithesis of everything we regard as distinctively eighteenth century. His rigorous asceticism in his own life, his states of ecstasy and mystical prayer, and his utter unworldliness would have been repulsive, if not altogether incomprehensible, to those cultivated ladies of the Paris salons or the witty and amusing gentlemen in London coffee houses discussing political corruption or, in more serious mood, the "rational" religious ideas of Mr. Locke. Their dislike of "enthusiasm" would have found no supporting echo in the life of the Passionist founder.

Our second exemplar of eighteenth-century otherworldliness is the founder of another modern preaching congregation noted for austerity and zeal like that of the Passionists. Alfonso Maria dei Liguori (St. Alphonsus Liguori) was born near Naples four years before the end of the seventeenth century. When he died (1787) at the age of ninety-one the beginning of the French Revolution was only two years away, so that his long life virtually spans the "dismal" eighteenth century, as Baron von Hügel called it. His religious foundation, the Congregation of the Most Holy Redeemer (Redemptorists) was especially committed to the spiritual care of a very neglected section of the Italian population, the rural poor. His own predilection was for work among the goatherds in the mountain regions. Forgetting his aristocratic birth and the legal profession in which he had started a career, he sought obscurity and the humblest kind of priestly work with his ascetic Redemptorists. He refused an important archbishopric, that of Palermo, but was prevailed on finally to accept a poor and remote diocese in southern Italy. Devout Catholics, more especially in the Latin countries, know him as the author of a book of Marian devotion, *The Glories of Mary*. In seminaries and religious houses of study he is an authority on moral theology. Like other saints noted for their personal austerity, he seems to have had a singularly gentle and winning personality; of many delightful details recorded by his biographers perhaps the most significant is that at the end of a very long life of priestly work, which must have included the hearing of innumerable confessions, he could say that he had never dismissed a penitent unabsolved.

The fragmentary Jesuit order surviving in Prussia and White Russia managed to preserve the form and the spirit of Ignatian life while these teachers and missioners awaited better times and the restoration of their order. There were, besides this, experiments in setting up associations similar in spirit and aims to the Society of Jesus. One of these was the Society of the Most Sacred Heart of Jesus. It began in Belgium and when driven out by the French Revolution settled in Austria. Although it had but a brief existence it holds an important place in the modern history of the Church. One of its members was Father Joseph Varin, who became a Jesuit when the Society was restored by Rome. His scholarship and his skill as a spiritual director, a somewhat severe one, might not of themselves suffice to keep his memory alive. As in the case of other devoted teachers who have been outshone by brilliant pupils, we recall Father Varin because he formed and trained a modern saint whose name stands out in the history of education. This was St. Madeleine Sophie Barat, foundress of the Ladies of the Sacred Heart.

15. The Church's Loss and Gain in the Nineteenth Century

1. Pope Pius VI, then in his eighty-second year and a prisoner in the hands of the French, died in the last year of the eighteenth century. He had grown to maturity and old age, faithfully serving the Church for a lifetime, in a world that had passed away forever. A new world had arisen in North America and, with more violence and bloodshed, in France during his pontificate. Pius VI did not accept it; circumstances were against his coming to terms with it. When a French embassy official had been murdered in papal Rome, French revolutionary troops had occupied the city and set up a republic. The pope's refusal to forswear his temporal rights led to his arrest and his transfer from place to place until his last illness in the old town of Valence on the river Rhone. Perhaps during the last weeks of August 1799 the dying pontiff thought about the century about to begin. It is likely his thoughts were gloomy ones. He was dying too soon for an historical perspective which would show that the two revolutions, the American and the French, had served the Catholic Church by sweeping away royal absolutism.

A survey of the years between 1800, when the Benedictine cardinal Chiaramonte became Pope Pius VII, and 1903, when Leo XIII died, shows us the Church under attack in various countries, her ruler despoiled of territory and temporal authority, her teaching assailed by intellectual forces based on new theories in science and economics. The lapse of the first half of our present century has enabled us to see that the pontificates of the six popes who ruled the Church in the nineteenth century comprise an era of religious enterprise and of spiritual vigor for which we must go back several centuries to find a parallel. Much that ceased to be valuable was discarded; sources of intellectual strength that had lain idle were brought into use again. Above all, especially under Pope Leo XIII (1878-1903), the Church was truly the Church Militant, winning respect even where there was no love. The nineteenth century was for the Catholic Church a time of vast material loss and incalculable spiritual gain.

The alternation of action and reaction in human affairs had given the world the French Revolution followed by the dictatorship of Napoleon Bonaparte. Pius VII and Napoleon established an uneasy peace between the Church and revolutionary France in the concordat signed in 1802. Napoleon's religion was a doubtful quantity, but in his new role he needed Catholic support. The concordat was acceptable to the pope; Napoleon's subsequent additions to it were not, added as they were without the pope's consultation or consent. Pius refused to sign them. Thus began his travels under coercion which have given him the title of *Papa peregrinus* (the Pilgrim Pope). He crowned the emperor in Paris, but further disagreements, about French attacks on papal territory and the papal condemnation of the emperor's self-decreed divorce, led to Pius's imprisonment at Fontainebleau. Another concordat was signed, but on second thoughts the pope repudiated it as a concession to tyranny and remained Napoleon's prisoner until freed by the emperor's abdication in 1814 and his retirement to the island of Elba.

During his captivity the pope resolved on an act of great importance to the Church, especially in her educational and missionary work. With the aid and encouragement of Cardinal Pacca, his friend and fellow prisoner, he planned the restoration of the Jesuits, which took place as soon as he was back in Rome.

The final defeat of Napoleon at Waterloo in 1815, after his temporary return to power in France, and his exile to St. Helena were followed by the efforts of the statesmen at the Congress of Vienna to turn back the hands of the clock. The Bourbons were put back in power, Louis XVIII in France, Ferdinand VII in Spain and Ferdinand I, later King of the Two Sicilies, in Naples. To the pope who had suffered insult, spoliation, and captivity at Napoleon's hands there could be no alternative to supporting the Catholic Bourbons, despite their record of absolutism.

2. The spiritual prerogatives of the successors of St. Peter do not include second sight or the gift of prophecy. We, looking back over the years, may see a special significance in the birthdays of two men while Pius VII was pope. Both would come to symbolize two major influences of our present world—an active, intellectualized Christianity with the pope as its leading spokesman and, on the other hand, Christianity's most formidable enemy, Marxist communism.

In 1801 a London businessman had his baby son christened in the Church of England under the name of John Henry Newman. Seventeen years later a son was born to a Jewish lawyer in Rhenish Prussia. When he was six years old little Karl Marx was baptized a Protestant Christian along with the rest of his family.

An event that at the time seemed unimportant except

to the small enclave of hereditary English Catholics was the passing of the Catholic Emancipation Act in 1829. From the dwindling body of "old," that is, hereditary, Catholics in George IV's kingdom this removed most, but not all, of the civil disabilities they had borne so long. Although the wave of conversions and the mass immigration of Irish Catholics driven abroad by the potato famine were events a dozen years away, there was a rapid increase in the number of Catholics in England.

A few years later—Newman assigns the year 1833—there began something that was to be of great moment to the English-speaking portion of the Catholic Church, namely, the Oxford Movement, known at the time as the Tractarian Movement. As the Tractarians, whose leadership had passed from Dr. Pusey to the younger and more stimulating John Henry Newman, steadily undermined their Protestant heritage and moved, however reluctantly, Romewards, papal Rome herself looked on hopefully and it may be prayerfully, but was puzzled by the English mind. Ecclesiastics in Rome cherished the story of an eminent cardinal-theologian's outburst. Mystified by Dr. Newman's hesitations, intuitions, and apparent distrust of formal logic, but approving the more scholastic cast of mind of one Reverend William Palmer, now forgotten except by students of England's religious history, he exclaimed, *"Optime, ille Palmer! Newmannus miscet et confundit omnia!"* ("Well done, Palmer! Newman mixes up and confuses everything!").

A dozen years after the Oxford Movement had begun, Newman, in Disraeli's vivid phrase, struck the blow "under which the Establishment still reels," for on a stormy October night in 1845 he submitted to Rome at the feet of the Italian Passionist missioner Father Dominic. Thus the Catholic Church acquired her greatest modern defender and apologist in the English tongue. Other converts followed Newman and, less tactfully than he, sought to galvanize the "old" English Catholics into propagandist activity and, at times, provoked understandable irritation. The most famous convert after Newman was the Anglican archdeacon of Chichester who became Cardinal Manning. He was received into the Catholic Church in 1850. His friend, Frederick William Faber, together with Newman introduced St. Philip Neri's Congregation of the Oratory into England, but thereafter the two converts went their own ways. Newman, tactful, conservative, essentially English, established his community in the Midlands; Faber, exuberant, romantic, Italianate, in London. English Catholicism would be the poorer had she lost either of these two converts. Newman, of course, is a permanent addition to the literature of the English-speaking world. Faber's hymns, whatever their literary value, are still used as an aid to devotion, wherever Catholics speak English. Wordsworth saw a great poet lost to England when Faber became a Catholic; readers of poetry are still puzzled by Wordsworth's judgment.

Five years after Newman's conversion it seemed to Pius IX, who had become pope in 1846, that the time was ripe to reestablish the hierarchy in England. Since the Reformation the country had been a missionary area under the Congregation of Propaganda, with her Catholic population ruled by vicars-apostolic. Pius IX gave the cardinal's hat to Dr. Nicholas Patrick Wiseman, at that time coadjutor-bishop to one of the vicars-apostolic, and told him he was to be head of the new hierarchy as archbishop of Westminster.

Wiseman was one of those cosmopolitan Englishmen who are untrue to what is regarded as the general type. He was of Anglo-Irish parentage, Spanish birth, Italian education, was a polyglot scholar, and possessed a bubbling enthusiasm derived from his Irish parent or his Mediterranean nurture. To the small, unobtrusive body of "old" Catholics in England and the great mass of their diehard Protestant countrymen, he announced the impending new order of things in his first—and most flamboyant—pastoral letter, "From out of the Flaminian Gate." The plump, erudite, good-natured cardinal was tremendously taken aback by the fierce "Papal aggression" riots in which windows were smashed, bonfires lighted in the streets, and pope and new cardinal-archbishop burned in effigy. Wiseman was equal to the occasion. His own personal charm and his sincere and temperate *Appeal to the English People* were oil on troubled waters. The storm subsided as quickly as it had arisen. Soon distinguished Englishmen, lay and clerical, were eager guests at the cardinal's dinner parties in Golden Square. Wiseman was a good friend to the new converts as well as the "old" Catholics, and his diplomacy served to unite both groups in the common effort as well as to allay Protestant suspicion. When he died in 1865, Londoners turned out in their tens of thousands to line the streets and honor his funeral.

A wave of hopefulness, oversanguine as the event proved, was passing over the Church in the years just before the middle of the century. Catholicism in Germany, with a great prelate, Bishop Ketteler, as its inspiration, was enjoying a renaissance. In England the Catholics, especially the converts, were dreaming of a "second spring" to precede a corporate return of Anglicans to Roman unity. French Gallicanism had been weakened and largely discredited by a remarkable man who himself seceded from the Church when he had done his best work. The Abbé Felicité Robert de Lamennais had left the Church and indeed ceased to call himself a Christian about 1834, but his former friends and allies, Montalembert and Lacordaire, restorer of the Dominican order in France, seemed to be preparing a happy marriage between orthodox Catholic faith and the new political democracy, together with an awakened social conscience.

3.   A similar thing was happening in Italy. The Risorgimento had not yet become antipapal and anticlerical. The intellectuals of the Italian nationalist movement were talking of a United Italy under the presidency of Pope Pius IX; mobs in the streets of Rome cheered Pio Nono as the *Papa-Re* (the Pope-King) who would help them to throw the hated Austrians out of Italy. Pius, however, hesitated, decided on neutrality, and disappointed his too-impetuous citizens.

In 1848, the year of Marx and Engels's *Communist Manifesto,* and a year of revolutions, there was rioting in Rome. Pius fled to Gaeta, and that winter the anticlericals set up their short-lived Roman Republic. It lasted until the following summer and then was put down by an army sent by Napoleon III. Pope Pius, kindly, affectionate, and humorous by nature, but embittered by what had happened, reoccupied his throne, guarded by French bayonets. The Risorgimento was now frankly antipapal, and much of its membership was Masonic and anti-Christian. The nationalist movement had Mazzini as its able propagandist, Garibaldi as a dashing and competent military leader, while the shrewd, competent, and middle-of-the-road statesman, Count Cavour, prime minister of the Kingdom of Sardinia, was the directing brain.

The spiritual life of the Church, in these troublous years, no doubt pursued its own course, little touched by political upheavals. In 1858 the little peasant girl, St. Bernadette Soubirous, saw her vision of the Blessed Virgin in the cave at Lourdes. Some months later there died in France a country priest, badly educated, whimsical, terrifyingly ascetic in his own life, an alleged miracle worker and a genius in directing consciences. He was called Jean-Baptiste Vianney; we know him as the canonized Curé d'Ars.

In 1854 a great impetus had been given to Marian devo-

tion in the Church by the formal declaration of the doctrine of the Immaculate Conception of the Blessed Virgin
as an article of faith.

4. Pius IX, whose pontificate had begun with Italian
dreams of the welding of nationalism and Catholicism in
the person of the *Papa-Re,* had become suspicious of
things calling themselves "liberal." To warn the faithful
of tendencies he viewed as perils to the Christian scheme
of life, he issued in 1864 the encyclical *Quanta cura* and,
as appendix to it, the more famous, wildly attacked,
and often misunderstood *Syllabus* of eighty propositions
condemned as erroneous. "Liberalism," a vague entity
whether seen as religious or political, was anathematized
insofar as it implied or approved of the denial of supernatural motives and aimed at a complete secularization of
civic life. Pius did not impose any special course of action
on Catholics; still less did he support rebellion or nonco-
operation for the subjects of "liberal" governments. The
Jesuit periodical, *Civiltà Cattolica,* defended the *Syllabus*
against the outcry that it was an unconditional attack on
all contemporary thought, scientific research, and political
democracy. "Thesis" and "hypothesis" should be distinguished, said the Jesuits. The hypothesis was that of a
wholly secular, nontheistic (not atheistic) state. Theoreti-
cally, Catholics would reject this as an ideal, but as loyal
citizens they would tolerate it in practice, dealing with
particular problems as they arose, using the legal or con-
stitutional means at hand.

Perhaps it was unfortunate that the sweeping terms of
the *Syllabus* gave apparent ground for false hopes as well
as unnecessary apprehension about the Ecumenical Council which the pope summoned for the winter of 1869.
There were Catholics who hoped that the Council would
sternly restrict the field of research and speculation for
members of the Church. There were others who trembled

to think that it might do this. Both schools of thought—or emotion—may have been influenced by something that had happened ten years earlier. In 1859 Darwin's *The Origin of Species* had been published and had disturbed many orthodox Christian minds, more, it must be admitted, in the ranks of old-fashioned Protestantism than elsewhere, because Darwinism appeared to raise insuperable difficulties in accepting the literal inspiration of the Old Testament. Political events in Italy, moreover, suggested the possibility of a pronouncement on the pope's temporal power which would immeasurably widen the gulf between loyalty to the Holy See and Italian loyalty to the new united kingdom of Italy that could now be only a matter of time. In 1861 the Parliament of the new Italy of Victor Emmanuel, meeting in Florence, had declared that Rome was the official capital of the kingdom. The Kingdom of Italy now included all the peninsula except what was left of the Papal States and some northern areas still in Austrian hands. Garibaldi had even tried to seize Rome, but had been driven off by French forces.

When the council had assembled in Rome it was decided that the doctrine of papal infallibility should be part of the agenda. There were some—as it turned out, very few—prelates at the council who did not believe that papal infallibility was a doctrine of the Church. In the end, when the doctrine had been defined, there were no rebels in the council. A small number of clerics and laymen in Europe refused to accept the council's declaration and went into schism.

The true cleavage, therefore, was not a matter of faith. It was a difference of opinion on policy, almost, one might say, on politics. Many Catholics, including England's Dr. Newman, as he then was, and in France the great and revered bishop of Orléans, Dupanloup, thought the time not yet ripe for a definition of something which, after all, the Catholic world as a whole sincerely believed,* but which might add to the difficulties of the Church in her dealings with secular governments. These Catholics were the "inopportunists." Even among the "opportunists" who desired to see the doctrine defined, there was a clear division into "maximizers" and "minimizers." The maximizers, people like the famous Oxford convert W. G. Ward, who, in his own words, would have liked to see an infallible papal declaration on his breakfast table with *The Times* every morning, were, in the event, disappointed. The qualifying clauses as to the pope's speaking *ex cathedra,* that is, officially as Head and Doctor (Teacher) of the Church, on faith and morals fell far short of the dreams of Louis Veuillot, the French Catholic journalist, and others who wished to hear that *every* utterance of a pope was an infallible proposition binding Catholic consciences.

The later sessions of the council were held in an unquiet time. War had broken out between the France of Napoleon III and the militaristic kingdom of Prussia, directed by its prime minister of "Blood and Iron," Otto von Bismarck. In Italy the troops of Victor Emmanuel's government were already on papal territory and were advancing towards Rome.

Soon after the departure of the assembled bishops the invading troops had reached the walls of Rome. The pope had asked that only a token resistance should be made, but his loyal papal troops fought bitterly against overwhelming numbers. Only Pius's strict order for surrender ended the tragic loss of life at the Porta Pia on September

---

* Pius IX's *personal* definition of the doctrine of the Immaculate Conception of the Blessed Virgin (1854) had been accepted without demur throughout the Church, for the simple reason that Catholics generally regarded the doctrine as one implicit in the "deposit of faith" committed to the Church by Christ.

20, 1870. Thereafter Pius and his successors until 1929 were the "prisoners of the Vatican."

Most of the evils foretold by the inopportunists failed to appear. Among the small number of Catholics who stood out against acceptance of the definition of infallibility as a doctrine and went into schism, the most famous was the German church historian Dr. Döllinger. He did not, as is often supposed, wish to be regarded as leader of the Old Catholic schism. In France the popular preacher and Carmelite priest Charles Loyson, known as Père Hyacinthe, refused to accept the definition, left the Church and lived in London for some years, married an Englishwoman, and then set up an Old Catholic church in Paris. He died in his eighty-fifth year in 1912.

Of political repercussions the most serious was the *Kulturkampf* in Germany, a quarrel between German Catholics and Bismarck, who attacked the Church, ably led by Bishop Ketteler, for the so-called divided allegiance of her members. Bismarck's ideas in this matter were akin to those of totalitarian states today. The fight dragged on with diminishing violence for more than ten years, until the Iron Chancellor was glad to make peace, having found, as the French say, that "Whoever eats the pope, dies of it."

Pius IX's pontificate was the longest in papal history so far—the thirty-two years between 1846 and 1878. In his later years he had to witness a good deal of friction between the Church and the modern ultranationalistic states. In Italy there existed the depressing stalemate between himself as pontiff and the king of an officially outlawed government.

5. There was, happily, another facet of the life of the Church which made of the nineteenth century a time of growth and vigor. Very markedly it was an age of missionary enterprise. This is true of separated Christians as

well as of the Catholic Church. The long reign of Victoria, who was crowned queen nine years before Cardinal Mastai-Ferretti became Pope Pius IX and who survived him by nearly a quarter of a century, was the great era of Protestant missionary undertakings. From England and Scotland there was a steady exodus of missionaries, of the Anglican and Free Churches, and too often their well-meant labors included the effort to win over neglected or ignorant Catholics in foreign lands. Catholic missionary institutes similarly were sending every year an increasing number of young priests to lonely or perilous outposts of the Church in Asia, Africa, and the wilder parts of both Americas. The older religious orders whose rules provided for foreign missions sent their young men regularly. The restored Society of Jesus was again taking an active part in the work. The Paris *Missions Étrangères,* a voluntary association but not a religious order, was not behind the orders in zeal, enterprise, and the self-sacrifice of its members.

One of the most remarkable, as well as the most picturesque of missionary foundations, is that of the White Fathers, the Society of Missionaries of Africa, devoted to work in north and central Africa, especially among the suspicious and intractable Mohammedan tribesmen. Cardinal Lavigerie, who organized these truly dedicated men, was a dynamic force in French Catholic life. He was archbishop of Algiers, with jurisdiction over all of French Africa. He was a strenuous worker for the total abolition of slavery and the slave trade. He threw himself with energy and enthusiasm into the campaign to persuade French Catholics to forget their squabbles about Bonapartist and Orleanist claimants to the nonexistent French crown and to take part as republican citizens in fighting anticlericalism and militant atheism in their country.

England, despite the smallness of her Catholic population, made her contribution to the missionary effort. The

English Society of St. Joseph at Mill Hill, north of London, undertook work on lines similar to the Paris institute of the *Missions Étrangères*.

Catholic education was very much in evidence during this time. The Jesuits had taken up the work, a major feature of their vocation, when they were restored in 1814, and all through the nineteenth century were opening schools and colleges wherever their numbers made it possible. In mid-century a Piedmontese priest-schoolmaster devoted himself with great success to work among boys in Turin and in 1841 established his Salesian teaching congregation for service at home and in the foreign missions. He was canonized, as St. John Bosco, by Pius XI in 1934.

Two of the older religious orders of the Church owe a great deal to a couple of remarkable French ecclesiastics who flourished in the nineteenth century. Father Lacordaire, whose name is almost a symbol for pulpit eloquence, restored the Order of Preachers (Dominicans) in France as a means of re-Christianizing sections of the population, especially among the industrial proletariat, that had become estranged from the Church. Benedictinism, so prominent a feature of French life before the Revolution, was moribund in nineteenth-century France until it was revived by the Abbot Guéranger. Dom Guéranger's influence extended also to the laity through his writings. Until he began his work of educating Catholics in the liturgical worship of the Church, the spiritual as well as the purely artistic treasures of the western liturgy had become a forgotten thing for most of the faithful.

6. With the last quarter of the nineteenth century is associated one of the most fruitful of pontificates in the long history of the Catholic Church. In the late winter of 1878, after the death of the beloved Pio Nono, the assembled cardinals elected as pope Cardinal Pecci, a scholarly ecclesiastic with much administrative and diplomatic ex-

perience. He took the title of Leo XIII. Gioacchino Pecci had been ordained a priest in the year Queen Victoria ascended the English throne, 1837. When, after a quarter of a century as pope, he died in 1903, the Catholic Church had undergone a transformation something like that of the fifteen years when Paul III was pontiff (1534-1549). Clerical education had been overhauled, organized and —no paradox, although it sounds like one—brought up to date by being taken back to its greatest source of nurture in the Middle Ages, Thomist scholasticism. Catholics the world over, lay and clerical, had developed a new and more sensitive social conscience, stimulated by Leo XIII's encyclicals. The bitterness of the *Kulturkampf* in Germany had been replaced by good relations between the Papacy and the new German empire. A great French cardinal had done his best, with Rome's hearty approval, to lead French Catholics to take part in the political life of their country.

In the English-speaking countries Catholicism made great progress in numbers and prestige. This was an important matter in a world wherein a quarter of the world's habitable land was still under British rule and English the most widely distributed of all languages. The growth of the Church in the United States within the period between the Declaration of Independence and the time of Leo XIII forms one of the most striking chapters in the story of the Catholic Church throughout her two thousand years of existence.

The new pope, Leo XIII, lost no time in dealing with the reform of priestly education. The year after his accession he issued the encyclical *Aeterni Patris,* which ordered that the training in philosophy and theology of all Catholic clergy should be based solidly on the works of St. Thomas Aquinas. Leo when a young priest had won his own doctorate in theology as a student of the great medieval Doctor, but it is worth noting that he was also a scholar in the humanist tradition—a graceful writer of Latin verse and of Latin prose in the best Ciceronian style. Thomist doctrine, however, was his great intellectual interest. He founded an institute for its study at the Belgian university of Louvain and initiated the scholarly edition of St. Thomas's writings known as the Leonine edition. Later in his pontificate he sponsored various Catholic enterprises in higher education, including the Catholic University at Washington, D.C.

The year 1879, when the encyclical *Aeterni Patris* was issued, also saw the award of the cardinal's hat to John Henry Newman, the aging genius living in semiretirement among his Oratorians in the English Midlands. Newman's sensitive spirit had been wounded by long years of neglect by his superiors in the hierarchy and by intrigue on the part of one or two ecclesiastical busybodies. When the pope gave him the highest mark of favor in his power there was general rejoicing in England on the part of Catholics and Protestants alike.

The stormy interlude of Bismarck's contest with the Catholic Church in Germany ended happily in 1887. Socialism had raised its head in the new Germany and the chancellor and his emperor needed allies. Who better than the Catholics? The anti-Catholic laws of the *Kulturkampf* were allowed to lapse and then were repealed. Leo diplomatically helped the settlement by arranging for two rather intransigent bishops to fade into a well-earned and honorable retirement. Finally friendship was confirmed at the jubilee of the emperor William I, thanks largely to the diplomacy of the papal nuncio whom the pope had sent to represent him at the celebration.

7. In France the strife was more prolonged, more bitter and, one has to admit, less creditable to many of the Catholics involved in it. Leo, reversing the policy of his predecessor, refused to condemn political liberalism. He

recognized that political democracy had come to stay and urged Catholics to play their part as citizens. The one exception he made was Italy, where the forcible seizure of papal territory had created a situation unparalleled elsewhere. Unhappily, in France the pope's words fell mostly on deaf ears.

Catholic royalism played into the hands of the opponents of the Church, and the rallying cry "Clericalism, there is the enemy!" became as potent as Voltaire's "Wipe out the infamous thing!" in the eighteenth century. An all-out campaign was begun in 1880 with an attack on the Catholic schools and the religious orders. The Jesuits were expelled and their property seized. The other orders were given a breathing spell and then they, too, shared the fate of the Jesuits. All this, of course, was dictated by deep hostility to the Church, and perhaps it is understandable that French Catholics of that era should have been mostly royalist, seeing in the restoration of the throne the hope of setting up the altar again. In the nineties, however, came what may justly be called a deplorable piece of folly and malice on the part of many French Catholics, especially those of the aristocracy and the upper ranks in the Church and the army.

Captain Dreyfus, a Jewish officer, was accused of selling military secrets to a foreign power. He was tried, convicted, cashiered, and sent to the penal settlement in French Guiana. Suspicion, however, soon centered on other officers, notably one Esterhazy, who eventually turned out to be the real traitor. Widespread demands for a fuller enquiry were met by a venomously anti-Jewish outcry, chiefly, one records with shame, from Catholic sources, including a periodical, *La Croix,* edited by a priest in a religious order. All this was very satisfactory as ammunition for the enemies of the Church, especially when Captain Dreyfus had been proved the victim of a conspiracy and restored to his rank in the army. Pope Leo

XIII was deeply distressed by the whole shameful incident and especially by the odium incurred by priests and bishops who had joined their voices to those of the hysterical anti-Semites.

8. If we seek to weigh the progress made by the Church in the nineteenth century against the losses, in material goods or the allegiance of large sections of nominally Catholic populations in France, Italy, and elsewhere under the influence of modern secularism, we must needs take a look at her story in the United States. Here we truly may perceive the New World coming to redress the balance of the Old.

English-speaking Catholicism in what is now the United States had its beginnings in the work of Father Andrew White and his fellow Jesuits from England, who landed on the shores of Maryland with the pioneer settlers in 1634. The proprietary colony had been granted to George Calvert, the first Baron Baltimore, who had the courage to renounce high office and become a Catholic in Stuart times. His settlement was the first to accept religious toleration as a principle of government. Unhappily this was repudiated when the colony came under Protestant domination, but a tenuous tradition of English Catholicism survived under more or less penal conditions like those in England.

When happier times came in the late eighteenth century, Maryland had the first Catholic hierarchy in North America south of Canada. John Carroll of Upper Marlborough had joined the Jesuits in Europe, taught philosophy and theology, and had become a professed father of the Society of Jesus in 1771. Two years later came the papal suppression of the order. Father Carroll was unspeakably saddened by this, but he returned at once to Maryland and set to work as a mission priest. He was a good friend of Benjamin Franklin, whom he accompanied on the unsuccessful mission to gain the help of the French Canadians in the revolutionary movement in the English colonies.

Carroll, who, along with his kinsmen, was a strong supporter of the Declaration of Independence, persuaded Rome to withdraw the American colonies from the jurisdiction of the English vicars-apostolic. He was himself then appointed vicar-apostolic to care for the small American Catholic population. When American independence had been achieved, it was necessary to provide a bishop for the new republic and Carroll was called back to England to be consecrated. The ceremony took place in the comparative obscurity of a country gentleman's private chapel, that of Lulworth Castle, the seat of the Weld family (1790).

The new bishop's diocese was vast and, in those days of poor or nonexistent communications, unmanageable, more so than ever when immense areas had been added to it by the Louisiana Purchase. The new division of areas of jurisdiction made by Rome resulted in Carroll's becoming the first archbishop of Baltimore. He at once tackled the problem of providing for a well-trained and educated American clergy and invited the Sulpicians to open a seminary in Baltimore. Another of his gifts to posterity is the college which, after the restoration of the Jesuits, became Georgetown University. It was at Georgetown that the veteran prelate died in 1815 at the age of eighty. His latter years had often been saddened by the lack of sympathy and cooperation from some of the clergy he had invited from Europe, who found it hard to forget European ways and adapt themselves to the life of a new country.

The record of all that was done by this great American churchman is impressive, but we must look at the statistics of the American Catholic population then and now to see what has grown from his planting. In 1790, the year when he was made a bishop in rural Dorset in the south-west of England, there were about forty thousand Catholics in the newly independent United States of America. Within less than a decade of Archbishop Carroll's death the number was close to a quarter of a million. Then, in the middle of the century, the United States, like Great Britain, received a huge addition to the Catholic population because of the exodus from Ireland caused by the potato famine. By 1850, the year of the reestablished hierarchy in England, there were over one and a quarter million Catholics in the United States in what, sixty years earlier, had been a single diocese. At the end of the century the estimated number was thirteen and a half million; at the present time it is about thirty-nine and a half million.

Of various nineteenth-century enterprises wherein a traditional Catholic activity is animated by typically American initiative, the founding of the Paulists (Missionary Congregation of St. Paul) is outstanding. The founder, Isaac Hecker, born of German immigrant parents, was largely self-educated. In his young days he was already a "seeker" and for a time shared the plain living and high thinking of the Brook Farm transcendentalists in Massachusetts. At the age of twenty-five he found his spiritual home in the Catholic Church. There was a vein of asceticism and mystical piety united to the German thoroughness and the acquired Yankee robustness in his character. He joined the Redemptorists in Europe and was ordained a priest by Cardinal Wiseman. The young Redemptorist's desire to see the Congregation established in America led to misunderstanding with its European head, and Hecker and four of his colleagues were released from their vows.

The proverbial convert's zeal made these young men desirous of Catholic propagandist work. Father Hecker had been distressed at having to leave the Redemptorists, but he quickly found an outlet for his zeal among his fellow Americans. Pius IX gave approval in 1858 to the new Congregation of St. Paul, priests living the religious life in community without vows and working particularly for the conversion of non-Catholics in North America. Like all founders, Father Hecker had his troubles. He did not claim to be a profound philosopher, and it may be that some of his utterances on the subject of "passive" and "active" virtues were somewhat at variance with Aristotelian and Thomist scholasticism. There was, moreover, a good deal of talk about a new and rather intangible heresy called "Americanism." The suspicions of ultraconservative churchmen about the new, active American missioners continued after Father Hecker's death and were formulated in a book by a French ecclesiastic, with the challenging title *Father Hecker; Is He a Saint?* The Paulists lived it all down and went on from strength to strength, preaching, writing, giving missions, setting new standards in Catholic journalism. Father Hecker had founded *The Catholic World* in the sixties and was its editor until his death in 1888.

9. Two features of the Catholic Church history of the late nineteenth century will strike anyone who delves into this era of intellectual and social ferment. It was an age of great papal encyclicals; secondly, it appears to be the point in history when the pope and his Curia first took stock of the significance of American Catholicism for the future of the Church. The two things are, perhaps, more closely connected than is at once apparent.

At the very outset of his pontificate Leo XIII had shown his determination to base Catholic philosophy, especially as part of the education of the clergy, on the teachings of Aristotle as assimilated to Christian belief by St. Thomas Aquinas. This was the point of the *Aeterni Patris* (1879). Less than ten years later the encyclical *Immortale Dei* dealt with the subject of authority in the state and the source of legitimate authority. The question of religious toleration, desirable and indeed inevitable in our modern "mixed" society, was the subject of another encyclical about this time. Finally, in 1891 we come to the greatest of all these papal documents, the classic *Rerum novarum,* issued in 1891. Sometimes known as "The Working Man's Encyclical," it is a treatise on the whole social problem in all its aspects—the obligations and acceptable mutual relations of capital and labor, the rights of workers to voluntary association and collective bargaining, and their ethical claim to a living wage and reasonable leisure. Monopoly capitalism and industrial slavery came under the papal condemnation as wholly as Marxist communism. Leo XIII does indeed speak with disapproval of "socialism," but it should be noted that he thus refers to the Marxism of the two Internationals, not to the Christian Democracy of modern Italy or France or the moderate section of the British Labor Party.

In the eighties, that is to say about ten years before the publication of *Rerum novarum,* events had been taking place in the United States which showed that Leo XIII was well aware of the just place of certain modern tendencies within the life of the Church. An energetic Catholic layman in the United States, Terence Powderly, was very conscious of two sinister threats to the Catholic working population of his country. In the first place, they, along with the rest of the workers for wages, had to carry on a steady fight against the so-called rugged individualism of big corporations and industrial magnates. The lack of efficient means to do this, as well as the natural desire of men for mutual help in a framework of social fellowship, was leading numbers of Catholics in industrial areas to disregard the ban of their Church on Masonic and other societies with secret oaths and initiations. Freemasons in America, as in Britain, were powerful, well organized, philanthropic, and altogether free of the anticlerical and even anti-Christian bias of the lodges in Latin Europe.

Powderly met the need with the establishment of his Knights of Labor, open to Americans of all beliefs but with a large Catholic membership from its earliest days. It bore a strong resemblance to our present-day A.F. of L. —C.I.O. organization. There was, of course, no secrecy; its declared objects were mutual benefit and collective bargaining. Nowadays it is inconceivable that it could be looked at askance by any Catholic cleric. The nineteenth-century hierarchy in Europe, however, saw all associations the least bit left of center as sharing the anti-Church spirit of Italian Masons and the secret, revolutionary Carbonari. Condemnation by Rome seemed to threaten the Knights of Labor in spite of the approval of leading Catholic bishops in the United States. Perhaps it was the voice of the beloved and widely popular archbishop of Baltimore, the future Cardinal Gibbons, that averted the blow. It is no exaggeration to say that all Terence Powderly believed in and worked for was summed up in *Rerum novarum*—in the excellent Latinity of Pope Leo XIII, who wrote his own encyclicals.

Leo, dying in the early years of the new century (July 20, 1903), left behind him a Church whose life and multifarious activities had been renewed like the Psalmist's youth—*ut aquila,* as an eagle. Critical times were ahead and Catholics will see a guiding Providence in a pontificate that built up reserves of spiritual strength and of initiative in all kinds of religious enterprise.

16. The Church in a Troubled
Twentieth Century

1. After the death of Pius IX in 1878 occurred the shameful incident when a Roman mob, stirred up by anticlericals, hurled insults at the pope's coffin as it was taken through the city at night. Mud was thrown at it, and there was an attempt to seize it and throw the pope's body into the Tiber. When Pius's successor, Leo XIII, died in 1903, there was universal expression of sympathy and respect. This seemed to augur well for civilization and the Church in the century that was still young. The twentieth century, however, has turned out to be a troublous one, and few believe that the end of the troubles is in sight.

A last relic of royal absolutism was swept away with the accession of the new pope. Before the conclave there had been speculation as to the chances for election of the Sicilian cardinal, Rampolla, a statesman and diplomat. Rampolla's allegedly liberal sympathies and his unconcealed Italian patriotism were uncongenial to the Austrian emperor Franz Joseph who, as residuary legatee of the Holy Roman Empire, claimed a veto on unacceptable candidates for the papal throne. Anyhow, the final ballot, with the requisite majority, was for Giuseppe Sarto, the cardinal who was patriarch of Venice. Cardinal Sarto, born into a peasant family in northern Italy, was neither politician nor philosopher, nor was he a great scholar like his predecessor. He was a saint and, above all else, a pastor and a guardian of faith and morals. As pope he promptly voided all claims of the Austro-Hungarian Empire to any voice in papal elections. Then, almost at once, he turned his attention to more serious matters. The new pope had chosen the title Pius X; he is now St. Pius X.

In the early years of the new pontificate a bitter persecution of the Church in France was going on. The year 1905 was that of the separation of church and state by an anti-Catholic government, which accompanied the legislation with the expulsion of the religious orders, the confiscation of their property, and the seizure of a large number of Catholic schools.

2. Back in the days when "Americanism," understood as a religious, not a political, term, was disturbing nervous ecclesiastics in Rome, there was talk of something called "Modernism." The word generally meant little more than certain activist and, in some nonessentials, untraditional features of American Catholicism, and must be distinguished from the later Modernism of the twentieth century, a heresy condemned as such and having little impact on North America.

The spirit of Modernism within the Church had made itself felt in the closing years of the nineteenth century and was especially associated with the eminent Biblical scholar, the Abbé Loisy, who ultimately was excommunicated and died outside the Church in 1940 at an advanced age. Loisy's academic record was impressive. He had studied under the learned church historian, Louis Duchesne, himself a pupil of Pellegrino Rossi, the outstanding authority on the Roman catacombs as source material for early church history. Loisy had, after his early studies, specialized in Biblical history and criticism and had developed a rationalistic and antisupernatural view of the New Testament documents and the growth of Christianity which went undetected for a time.

The aims of the Modernists were expressed by the best known of its English representatives, Father George Tyrrell, as "the desire and effort to find a new theological synthesis. . . . By a Modernist I mean a churchman of any sort who believes in the possibility of a synthesis between the essential truth of his religion and the essential truth of modernity." The heart of the matter is in the interpretation given to the word *essential* and in the seductive spell of *modernity*, a thing which of its nature is transitory. In justice to the Modernists, many of them learned and devout clerics and laymen, we must admit that their motive was often that of saving the faith and peace of mind of contemporary Catholics torn between loyalty to the Church's doctrine and an anguished sense that this was threatened by modern science.

That the movement was bound to lead to subjectivism and act as a solvent of all dogmatic religion gradually became clear. The Abbé Loisy's teachings were condemned by the Decree *Lamentabili.* The popular Italian writer Fogazzaro's novel *Il Santo* ("The Saint") was censured, but the author submitted and remained within the Church. Don Romolo Murri, an Italian priest-politician, tried to reconcile Catholic doctrine and Marxism. He refused to retract and left the Church, although he seems to have recanted later in life. Father Tyrrell, the brilliant Irish writer who had been a member of the English Province of the Jesuit order, was excommunicated, but in his last illness was absolved and given Extreme Unction.

The condemnation of Modernist teaching, as summarized in sixty-five propositions, was contained in the encyclical *Pascendi Dominici gregis* of 1907. There was an outcry, charging the pope with intransigence, arrogance, and obscurantism, but as the Protestant Dean Inge has pointed out, the pope could not logically do otherwise than ban a system of thought which undermined the whole fabric of Catholic belief. Many outsiders, as well as some Catholics, thought that Pius X was severe, even ruthless, in his condemnation of Modernism and in the disciplinary steps he ordered to forestall "burrowing from within" by professors in seminaries and other teaching institutions. These critics seemed unaware he was dealing with a subtle and insidious propaganda whose logical outcome was the agnosticism in which the Abbé Loisy ended.

3. In 1911, while some of the best minds in Europe were still busy with the reconciliation of faith and modern science and while others, who watched international affairs, were disturbed by the armament race, a little-publicized event took place up the Hudson River, some miles above New York. Very modestly the Catholic Foreign Mission Society of America, generally known as the Maryknoll Fathers, began operations and, seven years later, sent its first contingent of trained missionaries to the Far East. These priests, and a similar foundation of missionary sisters, form one of America's best-known contributions to the missionary effort of the modern Church. They have already had their quota of martyrs and confessors of the Faith in Communist China.

Certain features of Catholic life in the years just before the first world war are signs of the spiritual vitality to be expected when a saint wears the papal tiara. St. Pius X was, above all else, a pastor. Ecclesiastical legislation started or supported by him all looks toward fostering the Christian life. Some critics found it hard to reconcile the stern pope of the *Pascendi* encyclical with the kind and wholly charming pontiff in the Vatican. Better than his critics he saw faith threatened. The same pastoral solicitude underlay other enactments of these years. One of the most important for the spiritual life of the Church was the promotion of frequent communion and the early reception of the Eucharist by children. For the clergy and the more learned laymen there was new work on the liturgy, the Roman Breviary, and the Latin text of the Bible. Not to be overlooked, if one is old enough to recall the operatic displays which passed for sacred music, was a papal decree (*Motu proprio*) recalling Catholics to traditional church music.

A work started about the same time but held up for two years was the codification, that is, the reorganizing and editing, of the whole body of canon law. Through the centuries church legislation had piled up, often very haphazardly, until the task of reducing it to order seemed almost beyond the power of man. Various popes turned from the affair in desperation. St. Pius X decided to make a start. He summoned the experts, including the learned Jesuit canonist Father Wernz, who, two years later, became the general of his Society. Archbishop Gasparri, a future cardinal, was put in charge of the work and he was assisted by a young professor of canon law, Father Pacelli, the future cardinal who became Pope Pius XII. The *Codex* which was the outcome of these men's labors was published in 1917.

4. Poetical literature contains a great deal of fantasy woven about heroes and heroines who die of broken hearts. From time to time real life holds up the mirror to romance. Of the last illness of St. Pius X in the late summer of 1914, it is known that the end was hastened by the shock and bitter grief he suffered when war broke out on August 4. Another religious leader, whose position made him also the spiritual father of men on both sides, lay dying at the same time. The papal benediction of the dying pope was sent to the dying father-general of the Society of Jesus.

When wars were simpler in their origin—the whims or desires of power-hungry or land-hungry dynasts—the decision about a just or an unjust war was often easily made. A conscientious pope could proclaim the justice or injustice of an act of war and use the sanctions in his power, excommunication, interdict, and so forth, to punish the aggressor or protect the victim. Such is seldom the case with great upheavals like the two world wars, whose causes are complex, obscure, and elusive. The function of the Church in these global tragedies can only be that of the Good Samaritan, to bind up the wounds of the victims of war so far as possible.

Much calumnious nonsense was uttered about the "pro-German" attitude of the Papacy. In actual fact, as the records show, Pius X's successor, Benedict XV, the learned and humane Genoese cardinal who had been archbishop of Bologna, kept a scrupulous neutrality in a quarrel about many aspects of which the historians are still squabbling. Twice the pope made strenuous efforts to end the tragedy by pleading with the belligerents for a truce and subsequent negotiation. On both occasions he was rebuffed, first by the Allies, then by the Central Powers (Germany and Austria).

A less depressing part of the history of the first world war is that of the humanitarian work of the Papacy. The Vatican served as an international bureau whereby prisoners could get in touch with distraught relatives on both sides of the line of trenches that ran from the North Sea to Switzerland. Large sums of money, much of it from the pope's own treasury, were given to works of charity during the conflict and in the famine years that came after. Several times, protests were made to the German and Austrian governments about acts in violation of what is called civilized warfare.

5. The first world war ended in November 1918. Populations that had forgotten the horrors of war had hailed it in 1914 as a crusade; in the spring of 1917 the United States entered it with the rallying cry of making the world safe for democracy. Its legacy as seen in 1919 and the early twenties consisted of millions of starving and destitute people in defeated Germany; one great empire, Russia, overturned in a revolution marked by every kind of cruelty and disregard of human rights; another, Austria-Hungary, defeated and then broken up into embittered factions, the western Allies mourning some two million dead. The United States had suffered great losses in lives and money but was spared the worst horrors of Europe and Asia. The idealism of her wartime president was followed by the inanities of the jazz age and by corruption where there should have been world leadership.

The Catholic Church in the early postwar years carried on her duties to humanity with unobtrusive persistence. Large sums of money and the labor of many voluntary workers were devoted to the relief of suffering in countries laid waste by the war. Offers of help in money and manpower among the destitute and the homeless in the new Russian Soviet state were brusquely repulsed after a time; Russia's new rulers thought starvation preferable for their citizens to Rome's "opium."

The death of a Catholic saint usually passes unnoticed by the world at large and even by most Catholics until canonization brings the saint to general notice. Such was the case with the United States' first canonized saint. Mother Frances Xavier Cabrini, whose body is enshrined in New York City, died (December 1917) some months after her adopted country had entered the war. As a religious in northern Italy she had founded a congregation of nuns for work among the poor (the Missionary Sisters of the Sacred Heart) in schools, nurseries, orphanages, and hospitals. In 1889 she led a contingent of her nuns across the Atlantic to set up foundations in the Americas.

In Italy the course of events seemed to promise both religious and political salvation when Don Luigi Sturzo, a Sicilian priest, built up his *Partito Popolare* as a genuinely Catholic and democratic movement. Unhappily, Mussolini's *coup d'état*, his march on Rome, by Pullman car, and the surrender of the king to the Duce's threats made Don Sturzo's merely an opposition party, soon to be crushed and banned. While all this was taking place in Italy, the Church was being attacked in Mexico, where successive anti-Catholic governments carried out a policy of sequestration of property, banning of public worship, the exile of foreign clerics, and the imprisonment or execution of Mexican ones. These years gave several martyrs to the Mexican Church, the most famous of them Father Pro, the Jesuit. The story of his career of underground work in disguise as a mechanic, of hairbreadth escapes, final arrest, and death before a firing squad reads like an account of missionary-martyrs in Tudor or Stuart England.

One of the most vexatious features of church-state relations was the continuance of the "Roman question," that is, the position of the pope as the "prisoner of the Vatican" in the city seized by the invading forces in 1870. Until relations between the Papacy and the Italian government were amicably settled, Papal protocol regarded as an affront to the Vatican the visit of a head of state to the king of Italy, ruler of usurped Papal territory. This had led to bitter recrimination in France when the pope had protested against such a visit by the French president. In 1929 Pius XI brought this state of things to an end. His secretary of state, Cardinal Gasparri, signed with Mussolini as prime minister of Italy the Lateran Treaty. This established permanent relations between the Papacy and the Italian state. The tiny territory of 108 acres we know as Vatican City was recognized as a sovereign state, and the payment of indemnities by Italy was agreed on. It was a relatively modest sum, the pope accepting less than was offered.

The settlement was a statesmanlike move from which the Church has reaped the benefit in dealing with Italy herself and in easier contact with other governments. The treaty was not, as might have been feared by some people, a "deal" with Fascismo. Mussolini, of course, welcomed an arrangement that added to his prestige with a Catholic population, but he was too shrewd to demand any recognition by the pope of a totalitarian régime; this would have wrecked the success of the negotiations and weakened his position with Catholics generally.

Little time was needed to show the incompatibility of Catholicism and totalitarian rule. There were Fascist attacks on Catholic youth centers in Italy, brutal assaults on persons working in them, and the seizure of their equipment. An encyclical of the pope set clear limits to the collaboration possible between Fascismo and members of the Catholic Church. Peace was made, the seized property restored, and thereafter the Fascists behaved with reasonable "correctness." Hopes of a similar settlement in the new totalitarian Germany were soon proved vain. During the unhappy time of inflation and dire poverty under the Weimar Republic, the papal nuncio, Archbishop Pacelli, the future Pope Pius XII, had won general respect and he strove for an understanding that would ensure the freedom of the Church. In 1933, soon after Hitler had become chancellor, a concordat was signed. Almost at once the Nazis began to violate its terms, and this continued until a climax was reached in 1937 with the issue of the encyclical *Mit Brennender Sorge*, which was a denunciation of the whole Nazi philosophy. From then the Nazi party regarded Catholics as enemies and treated them as such. The position of the Church in the new Reich steadily worsened, particularly when the pope voiced his abhorrence of Nazi racialism and the persecution of Jewish Germans. After the seizure of Austria by Hitler, Catholics in that unhappy country suffered the same treatment as those in Germany, in spite of the misguided attempt of the archbishop of Vienna, Cardinal Innitzer, to come to terms—impetuously—with the Nazi invaders. The unfortunate cardinal had to suffer the humiliation of earning only the contempt of the Nazis and a stern rebuke from the pope.

In France, on the other hand, things had improved in the years preceding the second world war. Diplomatic relations with the Holy See were resumed; the "Cultural Associations" that had been devised to control the churches and their affairs in a frankly anti-Catholic spirit were replaced by new associations with Catholic members and were accepted by Rome. Across the Atlantic, too, there were brighter prospects, for the extreme anticlericals had ceased to control the government in Mexico and the clergy could once more go about their work in peace. Unhappily the drift towards another great war became increasingly observable, not least in the Vatican, always well informed about international affairs. The Spanish civil war called for much calm thought and courageous speaking on the part of church authorities. None but the self-deluded dreamers in various countries could fail to see that the Spanish Republic was being made a catspaw for Russian Communism and Italian Fascism to use in a trial of strength. Looking at the thing from the Spanish Nationalist side, however, there was less cause for satisfaction than some Catholics imagined. A Nationalist victory would almost certainly be followed by a dictatorship, and long experience had shown the Papacy that dictators, if they can, use the Church rather than serve her. Moreover, while the atrocities committed against Catholic churches, priests, and religious were many and abominable, atrocities were not limited to the Republican side. Well-informed Catholics, too, could not be blind to the horrors inflicted on the intensely Catholic, but Republican, Basques.

Despite all these sources of worry and unhappiness in the middle and late thirties, the Church went on her way as a missionary body with a divine command to "teach all nations." Visitors to the missionary exhibition set up in the Lateran palace were able to see something of the network of Catholic missionary enterprises, devoted to the physical and social as well as the religious welfare of native peoples. The headquarters of a great international organization, the Association for the Propagation of the Faith, had originally been established in France. Now, to emphasize its international character and for greater effectiveness, it was moved to Rome and entrusted with finding means to help the foreign missions, including the collection of alms throughout the world. Growing demands were made on the education of future missionaries as living conditions and social problems became more complex. The mission priest or brother often had to be diplomat, linguist, social worker, and research scientist as well as evangelist and minister of the sacraments.

The School of Oriental Studies set up in Rome had missionary needs in view, but it was intended also to aid an approach to the separated Christians of the various Eastern Orthodox bodies. Modern popes have given special care to the communities of Uniate Catholics in the Near and Middle East. These churches are in union with Rome but are deeply attached to the various eastern liturgies and to their own traditional practices. It had sometimes been found in the past that arbitrary efforts to make them conform to Roman usage in nonessentials had led to schism or their transfer of allegiance to the larger schismatic bodies in Russia and the Balkans. Any attempt to "Latinize" these Uniate Catholics has been strictly forbidden; indeed, there is now a policy, carried out chiefly through various religious orders, to ensure the steady supply of priests trained in the liturgical languages and the rites used by the Uniate Catholics.

6. Pius XI saw a threatened war drawing steadily closer and he did what he could to work for peace. "It is by force of reason, not of arms, that justice prevails," he said, and he made approaches to various governments through nuncios or apostolic delegates. Friendly replies were given by Britain, Belgium, and France, but Germany made it clear that anything from the Vatican was unacceptable. Pius XII who, as Cardinal Pacelli, was Pius XI's secretary of state, had been pope for more than half a year before the second world war broke out. The signing of the Moscow-Berlin Pact in the late summer of 1939 raised gloomy forebodings in the minds of Catholic students of world affairs. With the seizure of the Baltic republics by Soviet Russia and the second and more criminal partition of Poland, the worst had happened for Catholic Poland and for the large Catholic communities in the other states overrun by Soviet forces, especially Lithuania, where Catholics, both Latin and Uniate, had established a long tradition of culture and sound education. When hostilities had broken out, the Church, as in the first world war, could not hope to stop the conflagration; her efforts had to be concentrated on works of mercy and on preparation for a postwar world of unknown potentialities, mostly for evil.

In Hitler's Germany there was no longer even a pretense of official neutrality with regard to the Church and the clergy. Priests, monks, and nuns, along with lay men and women, were thrown into concentration camps.*

* In the early months of 1945, when the Allied armies were releasing Hitler's victims in concentration camps, there were nearly fifteen hundred

Frequently this was done as a punishment for sheltering or aiding the victims of anti-Jewish persecution. When Mussolini, taking his orders from Hitler and imitating the latter's policies, initiated a persecution of the Jews in a country which until then was remarkably free from this mania, Catholic clerics and religious found themselves victimized for helping Jews. At least one priest was shot for doing so. Two hundred Jews awaiting betrayal to the Gestapo, as prelude to extermination, were saved by the personal intervention of Pius XII, who contrived to hand over a large sum in gold to buy the release of the prisoners. In Rome the Vatican itself took on the aspect of a great relief station. Many fugitives found refuge there, and every day thousands of destitute people were fed and given the hope of survival that had seemed to be receding from them.

7. Of the years that have passed since the end of the second world war, no adequate history can be hoped for until time has established a clear perspective. The non-Catholic world has come to see clearly what was impressed on the Catholic consciousness a long time ago, that the Marxist philosophy is the enemy, not alone of Christian belief, but of all the social and political values we regard as distinctive of our western way of life. This enmity, however, is in many cases abandoning the old frontal attack of invective and denunciation. Where the Catholic population is ill-informed or suffering from poverty, low living standards, or industrial exploitation, communism assumes the disguise of a liberator and a good Samaritan. This has been the situation especially among the poverty-stricken peasants of southern Italy who, nominal Catholics anyhow, many of them genuinely devout, were ca-

---

priests in Dachau alone. Apparently one of Himmler's obsessions was a pathological hatred of Catholics, whom he had sworn to exterminate along with the Jews.

joled into voting Communist in the early postwar election. The story that the agents of Palmiro Togliatti won many votes by distributing "holy pictures" of St. Joseph backed by an exhortation to vote Communist for religion and a fair wage is, perhaps, apocryphal, but it illustrates a shrewd development of Communist strategy.

Marxist materialism as a philosophy is obviously incompatible with Catholic belief, but, in France and Italy especially, there were Catholic workers who thought that communism as a political party was acceptable as a means to social or economic reform. Many trade unions were largely Communist in membership, dominated by Marxist ideas and ardent in support of political communism. Romulo Murri, in earlier Modernist days, had talked of "Marxifying Christ." The infiltration of Communist teaching in Catholic sections of working-class society had reached a point in 1949 that called for a declaration by Rome that Catholics were forbidden to join the party or to aid in the defense and propagation of communism. An organization called the *Union of Christian Progressives* had set out as a nonparty association which repudiated atheistic materialism but claimed freedom to work with Communists in economic disputes and demands for changes in conditions of employment.

Another aspect of the tendency to the "left" as it affected Catholics has been the priest-worker movement in France. A number of priests in the industrial cities of northern France and around Paris had become appalled by the rapid de-Christianization of the working masses. The goal of these priests was to make closer contact with the workers by living among them, wearing their clothing, doing similar work part of the time, and joining their societies and unions. It was an idealistic plan, which won the respect of many people inside and outside the Catholic Church. The 1949 ruling by Rome that Catholics could not join the Communist party or Communist associations left in doubt the Communist-dominated unions. A definitive order forbade membership in the "C.G.T." (the French "General Confederation of Labor"). This large and powerful organization is Communist-dominated and largely Communist in membership. Rome moved slowly, tolerantly, not without sympathy, but by 1951 it seemed clear that the religious gain in the industrial proletariat was doubtful, whereas an undercurrent of Marxist thinking was showing itself among the clerics. The admission of recruits to the movement was suspended, and students in seminaries were forbidden to interrupt their studies by becoming apprentices to trades.

A crisis came in 1953, when the priest-workers joined in a manifesto backing the "C.G.T." against its opponents —the Catholic unions. Disquiet had already been caused in Rome when the ban on Catholic contributions to Communist periodicals was openly defied by a priest. An article in which he defended collaboration with the Communists was published in the Communist newspaper *L'Humanité.* The following year a large group—seventy-three—of the priest-workers rebelled against the restrictions on their activities. Three French cardinals visited Rome in 1954 for discussions on the subject. The outcome was permission to continue the priest-worker apostolate, but under closer episcopal control; it was also decided that careful provision must be made for normal priestly life. A small group of diehards in Paris lectured their archbishop on his responsibility and protested they had been victimized.

The winter that followed the temporary settlement of the priest-worker dispute was chosen for the inauguration of a Marian Year, starting on the feast of the Immaculate Conception of the Blessed Virgin (November 8). This was a logical pendant to the declaration in 1950 of the doctrine of the Assumption as an article of faith by Pope Pius XII, speaking *ex cathedra,* that is, in his official capacity as supreme pastor and infallible teacher of the Church.

The death of a popular monarch or head of a state always calls forth a widespread emotional reaction beyond the limits of his own jurisdiction. Much greater is this if the dead ruler was a respected religious leader. This was the case when Pius XII died in 1958. A great wave of popular sympathy, touching millions outside the Church he had ruled, was to be perceived in the press and in utterances by men in public life, often in quarters where traditionally Catholics seldom found much sympathy. The conclave that elected his successor, Pope John XXIII, would seem to have made a happy choice, if we may judge by the general affection and regard for a churchman who, before his election to the Papacy, was little known outside his own country.

Epilogue: The Future of the Catholic Church

To believe, as Catholics must do, that their Church cannot suffer extinction and, as they are free to do, to speculate on the outcome of certain present-day tendencies, may lead to bizarre and even contradictory forecasts. Some years ago a priest novelist, the late Msgr. Robert Hugh Benson, wrote two stories about an imagined future age of the Catholic Church. In one novel the Church had been ostracized, its membership had shrunk appallingly, and it was regarded only as a quaint relic by a de-Christianized generation. Western man had found a new god in a beneficent world dictator, a forerunner in less sinister form of "Big Brother" in George Orwell's *1984*. The other story depicted a victorious Church dominating our civilization, receiving and enforcing an obedience more absolute than in the Middle Ages. Had Msgr. Benson, who died in 1914, lived a few decades longer he might have added some brush strokes to both his pictures, but they would still be plausible.

It seems that in the Catholic Church today, whose membership as we near the closing decades of the twentieth century approaches 450 million, there is a higher average of religious practice than ever before. The sacraments are more often frequented by a larger percentage of her people and her laws more consistently obeyed than, perhaps, at any time since the Apostolic age.

The prevailing standards of priestly and monastic life, morally and intellectually, are very high. No previous century had run three quarters of its course under a more admirable group of pontiffs than those who have ruled the Church since the death of Leo XIII, himself one of the great men who have occupied the papal throne. All have been popes of exemplary life, one of them a canonized saint (St. Pius X, canonized September 1954), all of them ecclesiastics of administrative skill, several of them conspicuous for learning.

The modern Papacy, with a minute temporal kingdom of 108 acres and a military force of a few score men in obsolete but picturesque uniforms, has the respect of populations almost wholly outside the Roman obedience. "How many divisions can the pope put in the field?" Stalin asked contemptuously, but Communist parties and governments pay Catholicism the tribute of hating it; they are not so stupid as to despise it.

Many features of twentieth-century Catholicism, then, may encourage hopes that the Church will make steady progress in recovering the millions who are, nominally anyhow, Marxist unbelievers. That would inaugurate a religious Golden Age. On the other hand, because of the vast areas under totalitarian governments and in view of the technical and economic achievements of Soviet Russia, the Church is now face to face with an enemy of incalculable power and determination. The Papacy cannot, indeed, put a single division in the field and has explicitly vetoed the idea of an armed "crusade" against the Communist world, even were it practicable.

A feature of the spiritual militancy of the Church in our time is her strongly marked missionary character. At no earlier period were so many missionaries at work, both among the great industrial proletariats largely divorced from Christian belief and ethics and among peoples in Asia, Africa, and South America who have never been touched by Christianity or who drifted away from it because of the loss of teachers, as was the case in South America when the Jesuits were suppressed nearly two hundred years ago. Some of the missionary work remains unknown to the world at large, including most Catholics, because it is carried on in secrecy made necessary by persecution. Doubtless it has more martyrs in Communist countries than are yet on public record. An extension of this state of things, an underground Church as in the Roman Empire before Constantine, with legal proscription, arrest, imprisonment or exile, physical torture, may seem impossible in our western free world, although Hitler's Reich would have seemed impossible to Victorian liberals dreaming of inevitable progress and man's natural perfectibility.

There is one aspect of contemporary Catholicism that seems to justify a sober optimism. Increasingly the western world will come to figure in the Church's membership and administration. The time is drawing near when fully half the Catholics in the world will be living on the western side of the Atlantic. Of the Catholic population of the western world, somewhat less than half is in the predominantly English-speaking areas, the United States and Canada. Moreover, from North America comes the major contribution in money that enables the Church to carry on her work as an organized body, including vast missionary undertakings. This is encouraging, because the western countries generally accept the freedoms under which the modern Church can best do her work.

Lastly, there is encouragement in the decision of the new pontiff, John XXIII, to convene a twenty-first Ecumenical Council. His wish to make approaches to the various bodies of separated Christians, starting with the Eastern Orthodox churches, has been received with general sympathy and respect, even where skeptical voices question the outcome.

Index

Auxerre, 56
Averroes, 108
Avicenna, 108
Augustine of Canterbury, St., 60-2
Augustine of Hippo, St., 22, 38, 40, 42, 43-4, 54, 136, 179
Augustinus (Jansen), 180

"Babylonian Captivity," The, 114, 116
Bacon, Roger, 107
Baltimore, 211
Barat, M. S. *See* Madeleine Sophie Barat, St.
Barbarossa. *See* Frederick I, Emp.
Barberini Palace, 173
Baronius, Cesare, Cardinal, 170, 177
Bartholomew Massacre, St., 179
Bascio, Matteo di, 167
Basil the Great, St., 36-7, 48
Basilica, 126
Beatification, 86n
Bec, Abbey of, 99
Bellarmine, St. Robert, 170, 177, 184
Bembo, Pietro, Cardinal, 130
Benedict of Nursia, St., 49-51
Benedict V, Pope, 77
Benedict VI, Pope, 77
Benedict VIII, Pope, 80-1
Benedict IX, Pope, 81
Benedict XI, Pope, 113
Benedict XII, Pope, 115
Benedict XIV, Pope, 186
Benedict XV, Pope, 221
Benedictines, 206
Benedictus (monastic historian), 74
Benson, Msgr. R. H., 232
Bernadette, St., 200
Bernard of Clairvaux, St., 36, 80, 86-7, 90-6, 102, 104
Bernardine, St., 123

Bernis, Abbé and Cardinal de, 186
Bertha (Berta), Queen, 61
Berthold, 99-100
Berulle, Cardinal de, 176
Bishop, use of term, 15n
Bismarck, Otto von, 203-4
Black Death, 117
Bobbio, 60
Boleyn, Anne, 148, 150
Bonaventure, St., 105
Boniface VIII, Pope, 55, 62-3, 112-3
Borghese Palace, 172
Borgia (Borja), Lucrezia, 128
Borgia, Rodrigo. *See* Alexander VI, Pope
Boris of Bulgaria, King, 72
Borromeo, Charles. *See* Charles Borromeo, St.
Bosco, St. John, 206
Bossuet, Jacques B., Bishop, 183
Bramante, Donato d'Agnolo, 129, 130
Breakspear, N. *See* Adrian IV, Pope
Breviary, Roman, 220
Bridget of Ireland, St., 57
Bridget of Sweden, St., 117
Bruno, St., 79
Burckhardt, J., 144

Cabrini, Mother F. X. *See* Frances X. Cabrini, St.
Caerularius, Michael, 82
Cajetan, Cardinal (Thomas de Vio), 140
Cajetan, St., 155, 162
Calixtus III, Pope, 123
Callich. *See* Gall, St.
Calvert, George, Baron Baltimore, 210
Calvin, John, 136-7, 145-7, 178, 180
Camaldolese monks, 77-8
Campeggio, Lorenzo, Cardinal, 142, 149

Campion, Blessed Edmund, 168
Canada, 234
Canisius, St. Peter, 171
Cano, Melchior, O. P., 160
Canon Law. *See* Codex
Canossa, 84
Canterbury, 61
Canute, King, 67
Capuchins, 167
Carafa, Cardinal. *See* Paul IV, Pope
Cardinals, 83*n*
Carmelites, 100, 168, 177
Carroll, John, Archbishop, 210
Carthusians, 79
Casas, Bartholomew de las, Bishop, 174
Catacombs, Roman, 13, 18, 217
Cathari, 102
Cathedrals, Gothic, 99
Catherine of Aragon, 147-8, 150
Catherine of Russia, Empress, 189
Catherine of Siena, St., 116-9
Catholic, early use of term, 4, 6
Catholic Emancipation Act (England), 197
Catholic World, The (periodical), 213
Cavour, C. B., Count, 200
Celestine III, Pope, 97
Celestine IV, Pope, 106
Celestine V, St., Pope, 112
Celibacy, 101
"C.G.T." (French "General Confederation of Labor"), 230
Charity, Sisters of, 177
Charlemagne, 62, 69, 71-3
Charles V, Emp., 141-3, 157, 160, 162
Charles Borromeo, St., 164, 166, 172
Charles of Anjou, 107
China, 175
Choiseul, E. F., Duke of, 187
Chrysostom, John. *See* John Chrysostom, St.

Church Militant, Suffering, Triumphant, 10
Cicero, 38
Circumcision, 6, 9
Cistercians, 79, 80, 91
Citeaux. *See* Cistercians
Civiltà Cattolica (periodical), 201
Clairvaux, 91, 93, 94-5
Clare, St., 100, 101
Claver, Pedro. *See* Peter Claver, St.
Clement II, St., Pope, 81
Clement IV, Pope, 107
Clement V, Pope, 113, 114
Clement VI, Pope, 115
Clement VII, Pope, 141-2, 147, 149, 150
Clement VIII, Pope, 170
Clement IX, Pope, 181
Clement XI, Pope, 108
Clement XIII, Pope, 187, 191
Clement XIV, Pope, 189
Clement of Alexandria, St., 36-7
Clermont, 88
Clovis, 69, 71
Cluny, Cluniac Reform, 76-7, 78, 82, 98, 123
Codex (Canon law), 93, 220
Columba, St., 59
Colombière, Blessed Claude de la, 176
Columban (Columbanus), St., 59, 60
Columbus, Christopher, 127
Columcille. *See* Columba, St.
Contarini, Cardinal, 158
Corpus Christi, institution of Feast, 107
Corpus Christi, office, 107
"Conciliar theory," 123
Constantine I, Emp., 11, 12, 18, 20, 24, 34, 52
Constantinople, 27-8, 29, 30-1, 66, 68, 72, 82, 86, 122
Counter-reformation. *See* Reformation, Catholic
Cranmer, Thomas, 148, 150, 152